# Delicious
# Diabetes
# Cooking for
# One or Two People

# Delicious Diabetes Cooking
for
# One or Two People

## Michelle Berriedale-Johnson

Robert ROSE

Adapted from a book originally released by Grub Street Publishing.

*For complete cataloguing information, see page 144.*

**Disclaimer**
The recipes in this book have been carefully tested by our kitchen and our tasters.
To the best of our knowledge, they are safe and nutritious for ordinary use and
users. For those people with food or other allergies, or who have special food
requirements or health issues, please read the suggested contents of each recipe
carefully and determine whether or not they may create a problem for you. All
recipes are used at the risk of the consumer.

   We cannot be responsible for any hazards, loss or damage that may occur as
a result of any recipe use.

   For those with special needs, allergies, requirements or health problems, in
the event of any doubt, please contact your medical adviser prior to the use of
any recipe.

Design and production: Kevin Cockburn/PageWave Graphics Inc.
Indexer: Gillian Watts
Photographer: Michelle Garrett
Food styling: Jayne Cross

Cover images: Chicken Salad with Pumpkin Oil (page 42), Cracked Wheat with
Spinach and Pine Nuts (page 49), and Pears with Chocolate and Ginger Wine
Sauce (page 133)

The publisher gratefully acknowledges the financial support of our publishing
program by the Government of Canada through the Canada Book Fund.

Published by Robert Rose Inc.
120 Eglinton Avenue East, Suite 800, Toronto, Ontario, Canada M4P 1E2
Tel: (416) 322-6552 Fax: (416) 322-6936
www.robertrose.ca

Printed and bound in Canada

1  2  3  4  5  6  7  8  9  MI  22  21  20  19  18  17  16  15  14

# Contents

Introduction . . . . . . . . . . . . . . . . . . . . . . . . .7

• • •

Soups and Starters . . . . . . . . . . . . . . . . . .9

Salads and Vegetable Sides and Mains . . . . . . . . .27

Fish and Seafood . . . . . . . . . . . . . . . . . .53

Chicken and Eggs . . . . . . . . . . . . . . . . . .73

Pork, Beef and Lamb . . . . . . . . . . . . . . . . .91

Baked Goods and Desserts . . . . . . . . . . . . . . 111

• • •

About the Nutrient Analyses . . . . . . . . . . . . . 140

Index . . . . . . . . . . . . . . . . . . . . . . . . 141

# Introduction

WHATEVER OTHER MEASURES you may take to manage your diabetes, the bedrock of your treatment should be managing your diet. This means being aware of what you eat, how much of it you eat and, if you are insulin-dependent, when you eat it.

If your diet up to now has been heavily dependent on processed foods, it will also mean changing the way you eat. You may need to make a little extra effort in the kitchen, but you will end up eating much more delicious, much healthier food than you did before — and quite likely spending less money at the grocery store. The recipes in this book are designed to be easy to put together, to make this transition as stress-free as possible.

The recipes are designed for one or two people, but can easily be scaled up if you are entertaining (remember to increase ingredients such as cooking oil and seasoning slightly less than the main ingredients). I hope you will enjoy all the dishes so much that you want to eat them again; that way, even if you are on your own, recipes that make two servings will be welcome, as you can always freeze the remaining portion.

All of the recipes are made from "real" food, none are lengthy or complicated, and all are designed to encourage you to cook and experiment on your own, thus making cooking an exciting voyage of discovery rather than a chore. I hope you enjoy them.

# Soups and Starters

Leek and Fennel Soup. . . . . . . . . . . . . . . . . . . . . 10

Cream of Mushroom Soup . . . . . . . . . . . . . . . . 12

Watercress Soup . . . . . . . . . . . . . . . . . . . . 14

Carrot and Red Lentil Soup . . . . . . . . . . . . . . 15

Haddock Chowder. . . . . . . . . . . . . . . . . . . . 16

Celery Root Soup with Salmon . . . . . . . . . . . . . 18

Chicken and Lentil Soup . . . . . . . . . . . . . . . . 19

Chicken and Okra Savory . . . . . . . . . . . . . . . 20

Ajwar . . . . . . . . . . . . . . . . . . . . . . . . . . . 22

Eggs au Miroir . . . . . . . . . . . . . . . . . . . . . . 23

Hard-Cooked Eggs with Spinach. . . . . . . . . . . . 24

# Leek and Fennel Soup

This is a very simple, fresh-tasting soup, but if you want to make it more substantial, add the optional barley or brown rice.

| 2 | small bulbs fennel | 2 |
|---|---|---|
| 1 tbsp | olive oil | 15 mL |
| 2 | small leeks (white and light green parts only), trimmed and thinly sliced | 2 |
| ¼ cup | pearl barley or brown rice (optional) | 60 mL |
| 1½ tsp | soy or rice miso paste | 7 mL |
| 2 cups | water | 500 mL |
| | Freshly ground black pepper | |
| 2 cups | baby spinach leaves | 500 mL |

1. Trim fennel and cut into very fine slices. Set aside a few slices for garnish.

2. Heat the oil in a heavy pan and add the leeks and remaining fennel. Cook very gently, stirring often, for 10 minutes, then cover and sweat for 30 to 40 minutes.

3. Add the pearl barley or rice (if using). Whisk the miso paste into water, add to pot and bring to a boil. Cover and reduce to a simmer for 30 to 40 minutes.

4. Season to taste with pepper. Add spinach and let wilt in the heat of the soup. Serve garnished with fennel slices.

## NUTRIENTS PER SERVING

| | |
|---|---|
| Calories | 200 |
| Carbohydrate | 32 g |
| Fiber | 10 g |
| Protein | 5 g |
| Fat | 8 g |
| Saturated fat | 1 g |
| Cholesterol | 0 mg |
| Sodium | 301 mg |

**Food Choices**

1½ Fat

# Miso

Miso is a traditional Japanese paste made from fermented soy beans, rice or barley mixed with salt and fungus. There are hundreds of different varieties. Miso is used in cooking, as a soup (a staple of Japanese daily eating), in pickles and even in some sweet dishes. Apart from being delicious, it is also very nutritious, with high levels of zinc, manganese and copper and loads of protein: 2 grams for just 25 calories. However, it is also high in salt, so, when using miso, do not add extra salt until you have tasted the dish.

# Cream of Mushroom Soup

**Makes 2 servings**

This classic soup is improved by a hint of lemony sharpness.

## Tip

Look for a vegetable broth with less than 20 g of sodium per $\frac{2}{3}$ cup (150 mL), or make your own with no added salt.

### • Food processor or blender

| | | |
|---|---|---|
| 1 tbsp | olive oil | 15 mL |
| ½ | leek (white and light green parts only), thinly sliced | ½ |
| 8 oz | mushrooms, finely chopped | 250 g |
| | Juice of 1 large lemon | |
| 2 cups | no-salt-added or reduced-sodium ready-to-use vegetable broth | 500 mL |
| ½ cup | milk | 125 mL |
| Pinch | sea salt | Pinch |
| | Freshly ground black pepper | |
| | Several sprigs of fresh dill, chopped (optional) | |

1. Heat the oil in a heavy pan and heat the leek gently for 4 to 5 minutes or until it is starting to soften.

2. Add the mushrooms and continue to sweat gently, covered, for 10 minutes.

3. Add the lemon juice and the broth, bring to a boil and simmer, covered, for 10 to 15 minutes.

4. Remove 2 tbsp (30 mL) of the mushroom bits with a slotted spoon and set aside.

5. Purée the rest of the soup in a food processor or blender (how much will depend on how smooth you like your soup).

6. Return soup to the pan and add the cream. Season with a pinch of salt and with pepper to taste, then return the extra bits of mushroom to the soup for texture.

7. Serve sprinkled with chopped fresh dill, if desired.

## NUTRIENTS PER SERVING

| | |
|---|---|
| Calories | 159 |
| Carbohydrate | 15 g |
| Fiber | 2 g |
| Protein | 6 g |
| Fat | 9 g |
| Saturated fat | 2 g |
| Cholesterol | 6 mg |
| Sodium | 145 mg |

### Food Choices

| | |
|---|---|
| 2 | Fat |
| ½ | Extra |

# Mushrooms

Mushrooms are one of those great vegetables that have, effectively, no calories or fat, scarcely register on the glycemic index, yet still manage to pack a good deal of flavor and loads of nutrients, including vitamin C, riboflavin, niacin, pantothenic acid, iron, phosphorus, potassium, zinc, copper, manganese and selenium.

# Watercress Soup

**Makes 2 servings**

## Tip

Look for a vegetable broth with less than 20 g of sodium per $^2/_3$ cup (150 mL), or make your own with no added salt.

**● Food processor or blender**

| 2 | bunches fresh watercress | 2 |
|---|---|---|
| ½ | bulb fennel, trimmed and chopped | ½ |
| 2 cups | no-salt-added or reduced-sodium ready-to-use vegetable broth | 500 mL |
| 1 cup | drained rinsed canned white beans, such as navy (pea) or white kidney beans | 250 mL |
| 1 tbsp | pine nuts or sunflower seeds (optional) | 15 mL |
| Pinch | sea salt | Pinch |
| | Freshly ground black pepper | |

1. If you are serving the soup cold, reserve a few watercress leaves for decoration, then trim the thickest stalks off the watercress.

2. Place the watercress, fennel and broth in a large pan. Bring to a boil, then reduce heat and simmer for 20 minutes.

3. Add the beans and continue to simmer for 10 minutes.

4. Meanwhile toast the pine nuts or sunflower seeds under the broiler or in a dry frying pan until lightly browned.

5. Purée the soup in a food processor or blender, then return to the pan. Season with a pinch of salt and with pepper to taste.

6. If you wish to serve the soup hot, reheat and serve sprinkled with the pine nuts or seeds. If you wish to serve it cold, chill for a couple of hours, then serve decorated with the remaining watercress leaves.

## NUTRIENTS PER SERVING

| | |
|---|---|
| Calories | 210 |
| Carbohydrate | 35 g |
| Fiber | 8 g |
| Protein | 12 g |
| Fat | 3 g |
| Saturated fat | 0 g |
| Cholesterol | 0 mg |
| Sodium | 192 mg |

### Food Choices

| | |
|---|---|
| 1½ | Carbohydrate |
| 1 | Meat & Alternatives |
| ½ | Fat |

# Carrot and Red Lentil Soup

**Makes 2 servings**

Here's a North African soup with lots of flavor.

## Tips

Despite the fact that carrots and lentils seem starchy and filling, they both carry a low glycemic load, so you can enjoy this soup with a clear conscience.

Look for a vegetable broth with less than 20 g of sodium per $2/3$ cup (150 mL), or make your own with no added salt.

### NUTRIENTS PER SERVING

| | |
|---|---|
| Calories | 343 |
| Carbohydrate | 52 g |
| Fiber | 9 g |
| Protein | 19 g |
| Fat | 9 g |
| Saturated fat | 1 g |
| Cholesterol | 0 mg |
| Sodium | 132 mg |

**Food Choices**

| | |
|---|---|
| 2 | Carbohydrate |
| 2½ | Meat & Alternatives |
| 1 | Fat |

### Food processor or blender

| 1 tbsp | olive oil | 15 mL |
|---|---|---|
| 1 | large clove garlic, sliced | 1 |
| 1 tsp | ground cumin | 5 mL |
| ¼ tsp | ground coriander | 1 mL |
| 1 | carrot, sliced | 1 |
| ¾ cup | red lentils, rinsed | 175 mL |
| 1¾ cups | no-salt-added or reduced-sodium ready-to-use vegetable broth | 425 mL |
| Pinch | sea salt | Pinch |
| | Freshly ground black pepper | |
| | Juice of ½ lemon | |
| | Chopped fresh parsley (optional) | |

1. Heat the oil in a medium-sized, heavy pan and add the garlic, cumin and coriander. Stir and cook for 1 to 2 minutes, taking great care that it does not burn.

2. Add the carrots and continue to cook gently for a further 5 minutes.

3. Add the lentils and broth, bring to a boil, then reduce heat, cover and simmer for 35 to 40 minutes or until the carrots are quite tender.

4. Purée the soup in a food processor, then season with a pinch of salt and with pepper to taste.

5. To serve, reheat, add lemon juice to taste and sprinkle with parsley (if using).

# Haddock Chowder

This chowder is so substantial that you can enjoy it as a full meal. It tastes even better if you can make it a day in advance so that the flavors have time to mature.

| | | |
|---|---|---|
| ½ | small leek, trimmed and sliced | ½ |
| 2 | small new potatoes, halved or sliced | 2 |
| ½ cup | diced celery root | 125 mL |
| 1 | clove garlic, sliced | 1 |
| 1 | slice lemon | 1 |
| 2 cups | water, divided | 500 mL |
| ¼ cup | dry white wine (or 2 tbsp/30 mL white wine vinegar) | 60 mL |
| 4 oz | skinless haddock fillets or smoked haddock, cut into pieces | 125 g |
| 1 | tomato (fresh or canned), peeled and chopped | 1 |
| ½ cup | mixed dried seaweed, crumbled | 125 mL |
| Pinch | sea salt (optional) | Pinch |
| | Freshly ground black pepper | |

1. Place the leeks, potatoes, celery root, garlic and lemon in a wide pan with $1\frac{1}{3}$ cups (325 mL) of the water and the wine. Bring to a boil, then reduce heat and simmer briskly, uncovered, for 20 to 30 minutes or until the vegetables are tender.

2. Add the tomato and cook for 10 minutes. The liquid should be quite reduced.

3. Add the remaining water plus the seaweed, bring back to a boil and cook for 5 minutes.

4. Add the haddock and simmer for about 10 minutes or until fish is opaque and flakes easily when tested with a fork.

5. Season with a pinch of salt, if necessary (the seaweed may be enough) and with pepper to taste. Discard the lemon slice.

## NUTRIENTS PER SERVING

| | |
|---|---|
| Calories | 197 |
| Carbohydrate | 29 g |
| Fiber | 3 g |
| Protein | 15 g |
| Fat | 1 g |
| Saturated fat | 0 g |
| Cholesterol | 34 mg |
| Sodium | 292 mg |

### Food Choices

| | |
|---|---|
| 1 | Carbohydrate |
| 1½ | Meat & Alternatives |

# Seaweed

Seaweed, a staple of Japanese cooking, is very tasty, is highly nutritious and has a negligible glycemic load, so it is a great addition to any soup or salad, especially one that already contains fish. You can buy mixed packs of dried seaweed or sea vegetables in well-stocked grocery stores, Asian markets or health food stores.
Try using them as an alternative to your usual seasoning.

# Celery Root Soup with Salmon

**Makes 2 servings**

Though its ingredients are simple, this soup is really delicious. The salmon gives it a little edge — and turns it into a full meal — but you can make the soup with celery root alone, if you prefer.

## Tip

Look for a vegetable broth with less than 20 g of sodium per 2/3 cup (150 mL), or make your own with no added salt.

- **Food processor or blender**

| | | |
|---|---|---|
| 1 | small celery root (about 8 oz/250 g) | 1 |
| 1 | onion, chopped | 1 |
| 1¾ cups | no-salt-added or reduced-sodium ready-to-use vegetable broth | 425 mL |
| 6 tbsp | milk or non-dairy milk | 90 mL |
| ½ | can (7.5 oz/213 g) low-sodium salmon, drained, skin removed | ½ |
| Pinch | sea salt | Pinch |
| | Freshly ground black pepper | |

1. Scrub the celery root and peel off any earthy or green portions. Cut into large dice and add to a saucepan.

2. Add the onion and broth, bring to a boil, then reduce heat and simmer for 30 to 40 minutes or until the celery root is quite soft.

3. Purée the soup in a food processor or blender until smooth, then return to the pan over medium heat. Stir in milk and salmon and heat until steaming (do not let boil). Season with a pinch of salt and with pepper to taste.

**NUTRIENTS PER SERVING**

| | |
|---|---|
| Calories | 189 |
| Carbohydrate | 21 g |
| Fiber | 3 g |
| Protein | 15 g |
| Fat | 6 g |
| Saturated fat | 2 g |
| Cholesterol | 28 mg |
| Sodium | 290 mg |

**Food Choices**

1½  Meat & Alternatives

# Chicken and Lentil Soup

This is quite a substantial soup, and yields generous servings, so it would make an excellent meal on a cold winter's night. It also benefits from being cooked in advance to allow the flavors to mature — and it freezes well!

## Tip

Although lentils are carbohydrates, they are "good" carbohydrates, as they are an excellent source of protein, vitamins and minerals, especially folate and potassium, and a great source of fiber.

| | NUTRIENTS PER SERVING | |
|---|---|---|
| Calories | | 267 |
| Carbohydrate | | 4 g |
| Fiber | | 1 g |
| Protein | | 26 g |
| Fat | | 12 g |
| Saturated fat | | 2 g |
| Cholesterol | | 121 mg |
| Sodium | | 239 mg |
| **Food Choices** | | |
| 4 | Meat & Alternatives | |

| | | |
|---|---|---|
| 1 tbsp | olive or sunflower oil | 15 mL |
| 1 | stalk celery, finely chopped | 1 |
| 1 | slice ham, chopped small (optional) | 1 |
| 2 | chicken leg quarters, skin removed | 2 |
| 1 | bay leaf | 1 |
| 1 tsp | ground ginger | 5 mL |
| ½ tsp | dried thyme | 2 mL |
| ½ tsp | drained green peppercorns or black peppercorns, cracked | 2 mL |
| ¼ tsp | sea salt | 1 mL |
| 4 cups | water | 1 L |
| 6 tbsp | dry white wine (or 2 tbsp/30 mL white wine vinegar) | 90 mL |
| 2 tbsp | red lentils, rinsed | 30 mL |

1. Heat the oil in a deep pan and add the celery, ham (if using) and chicken. Sauté briskly for 10 to 15 minutes, stirring regularly to prevent the ingredients burning.

2. Stir in bay leaf, ginger, thyme, peppercorns, salt, water and wine. Bring slowly to a boil, cover and simmer gently for 1 hour.

3. Remove from the heat, let cool and remove the chicken bones. Pull the chicken meat into bite-sized pieces and set aside. Chill the soup thoroughly, then remove any excess fat, refrigerating chicken meat separately.

4. Return soup to the pan, add the lentils, bring back to a boil, then reduce heat and simmer for 30 minutes or until lentils are quite tender and virtually disintegrated. Return the chicken meat to the pan and heat through. Adjust seasoning to taste before serving.

# Chicken and Okra Savory

Serve this delicious little *bonne bouche* as a starter or pile it on toast and have it for lunch.

## Variation

Lay the lettuce leaves on a slice of whole-grain toast, then pile on the okra mixture.

| | | |
|---|---|---|
| 3 | pieces okra, uncooked | 3 |
| 1 | green onion | 1 |
| ½ cup | diced cooked chicken breast | 125 mL |
| 1 tbsp | olive oil | 15 mL |
| 1½ tsp | cider vinegar | 7 mL |
| Pinch | sea salt | Pinch |
| | Freshly ground black pepper | |
| 6 | leaves fresh basil | 6 |
| 4 | small lettuce leaves | 4 |

1. Trim the top off the okra and cut okra into thick slices.
2. Trim the green onion and thinly slice crosswise on a diagonal.
3. In a bowl, combine okra, green onion, chicken, oil, vinegar, salt and pepper to taste.
4. Chop 4 of the basil leaves and gently stir into okra mixture.
5. Lay the lettuce out on serving plates and pile the okra mixture in the middle. Decorate with the remaining basil leaves and serve.

**NUTRIENTS PER SERVING**

| | |
|---|---|
| Calories | 142 |
| Carbohydrate | 2 g |
| Fiber | 1 g |
| Protein | 14 g |
| Fat | 8 g |
| Saturated fat | 1 g |
| Cholesterol | 36 mg |
| Sodium | 251 mg |

**Food Choices**

| | |
|---|---|
| 2 | Meat & Alternatives |
| ½ | Fat |

# Okra

Okra is excellent for people with diabetes, as its gooey, mucilaginous juices are very helpful for blood sugar control. It is normally served cooked, but is delicious raw. Nicely crisp on the outside and soft inside, it does not taste remotely gooey and makes a great contrast to the soft chicken.

# Ajwar

Serve this delicious pâté with fresh whole-grain bread or toast, or as a dip with crudités. It keeps well in the fridge, so even if you are on your own, it is worth making enough for two.

## Tip

Both eggplant and peppers have negligible glycemic loads, so you can eat as much of this delicious pâté as you want.

| NUTRIENTS PER SERVING | |
|---|---|
| Calories | 164 |
| Carbohydrate | 20 g |
| Fiber | 6 g |
| Protein | 4 g |
| Fat | 8 g |
| Saturated fat | 1 g |
| Cholesterol | 0 mg |
| Sodium | 161 mg |

| Food Choices | |
|---|---|
| ½ | Carbohydrate |
| 1 | Fat |

• **Food processor**

| | | |
|---|---|---|
| 2 | thick slices eggplant | 2 |
| 1 tbsp | olive oil | 15 mL |
| 1 | large red bell pepper, roughly chopped | 1 |
| 1 | large clove garlic | 1 |
| 1 | thick slice whole-grain bread | 1 |
| Pinch | sea salt (optional) | Pinch |
| | Freshly ground black pepper | |

1. Fry the eggplant slices in the oil until they are just brown on each side.

2. Combine fried eggplant, red pepper, garlic and bread in a food processor and purée. The pâté should not be totally smooth when puréed; rather, it should have the texture of a country terrine.

3. Season with a pinch of salt and with pepper to taste. Let stand at room temperature for a couple of hours to allow the flavors to mature before serving.

## Ajwar

Ajwar is a Yugoslavian pâté made with the red peppers so beloved in southeastern Europe. Purists skin the peppers by submerging them in hot oil until they blister, and would look askance at the addition of eggplant, let alone whole-grain bread. However, skinning the peppers is a slow and fiddly business that is scarcely justified by the marginal improvement in flavor, and the pâté is so rich in its native form that a little "dilution" does not go amiss.

# Eggs au Miroir

Eighteenth-century cooks often combined orange and lemon juice with cream to achieve a rich dish that was not cloying — a very successful tactic! This unusual combination of flavors is based on an 18th-century recipe. You can enjoy it as a starter or as a light meal.

## Tip

Serve the eggs with whole-grain bread or toast and a green salad if you are having it as a main meal.

- **Preheat oven to 325°F (160°F)**
- **Baking dish**

| | | |
|---|---|---|
| 2 tsp | butter | 10 mL |
| 2 | green onions, finely chopped | 2 |
| 1 tbsp | finely chopped fresh parsley | 15 mL |
| 2 | large eggs | 2 |
| ¼ cup | heavy or whipping (35%) cream (or soy or oat cream) | 60 mL |
| | Juice of ½ small orange | |
| | Juice of ½ small lemon | |
| Pinch | sea salt | Pinch |
| | Freshly ground black pepper | |

1. Rub butter over the bottom of a baking dish large enough to hold the eggs and spread the green onions and parsley over it. Carefully break the eggs into the dish.

2. Mix the cream, orange juice and lemon juice. Season with a pinch of salt and with pepper to taste.

3. Pour the cream mixture over the eggs. Bake in preheated oven for 15 to 20 minutes or until the whites of the eggs are just set.

## NUTRIENTS PER SERVING

| | |
|---|---|
| Calories | 229 |
| Carbohydrate | 6 g |
| Fiber | 0 g |
| Protein | 7 g |
| Fat | 20 g |
| Saturated fat | 11 g |
| Cholesterol | 238 mg |
| Sodium | 199 mg |

### Food Choices

| | |
|---|---|
| 1 | Meat & Alternatives |
| 3½ | Fat |

# Hard-Cooked Eggs with Spinach

This very traditional combination is given a little edge by the slightly bitter Belgian endive.

| | | |
|---|---|---|
| 2 | large eggs | 2 |
| 4 cups | trimmed spinach (about 4 oz/125 g) | 1 L |
| 1 tbsp | good-quality olive oil | 15 mL |
| Pinch | sea salt | Pinch |
| | Freshly ground black pepper and ground nutmeg | |
| 1 tbsp | plain yogurt (cow's, goat's, sheep's or soy) | 15 mL |
| | Juice of 1/4 lemon | |
| 1/2 | head Belgian endive, trimmed and finely chopped | 1/2 |
| | Small bunch of fresh chives (or green onion tops), finely chopped | |

1. Hard-cook the eggs. When cooled, shell and slice.

2. Meanwhile, cook the spinach in 1/2 inch (1 cm) of water, then drain thoroughly. Stir in the olive oil and season with a pinch of salt and with pepper and nutmeg to taste.

3. In a bowl, mix the yogurt with the lemon juice. Mix in the endive and chives. Taste and season with additional pepper and nutmeg, if desired.

4. Arrange the spinach on a plate and place the sliced eggs in the middle. Spoon the dressing over top and serve immediately.

## NUTRIENTS PER SERVING

| | |
|---|---|
| Calories | 150 |
| Carbohydrate | 4 g |
| Fiber | 2 g |
| Protein | 8 g |
| Fat | 12 g |
| Saturated fat | 2 g |
| Cholesterol | 186 mg |
| Sodium | 197 mg |

### Food Choices

| | |
|---|---|
| 1 | Meat & Alternatives |
| 1 1/2 | Fat |

# Spinach

There are so few carbohydrates in spinach that they have no effect whatsoever on blood sugar — so you can eat as much of it as you like! Since it is also free of fat and cholesterol, but a good source of niacin, zinc, fiber, protein, vitamins A, $B_6$, C, E, K, thiamin, riboflavin, folate, calcium, iron, magnesium, phosphorus, potassium, copper and manganese, you should eat lots of it.

# Salads and Vegetable Sides and Mains

Brussels Sprout and Celery Root Salad . . . . . . . . . 28

Cauliflower and Cashew Salad . . . . . . . . . . . . . . . 29

Spinach, Avocado and Mozzarella Salad . . . . . . . . 30

Fennel and Strawberry Salad. . . . . . . . . . . . . . . 32

Spaghetti and Pine Nut Salad . . . . . . . . . . . . . . 33

Warm Pasta and Curly Kale Salad . . . . . . . . . . . 34

Beet and Chickpea Salad . . . . . . . . . . . . . . . . 36

Chicken and Apple Salad . . . . . . . . . . . . . . . 37

Pepper, Pear and Anchovy Salad. . . . . . . . . . . . 38

Fresh Seafood Salad . . . . . . . . . . . . . . . . . . . 40

Chicken Salad with Pumpkin Oil . . . . . . . . . . . 42

Red Cabbage Casserole . . . . . . . . . . . . . . . . 44

Kale with Beet Leaves . . . . . . . . . . . . . . . . . . 45

Celery Root with Kale and Pecans. . . . . . . . . . . 46

Ratatouille with Butternut Squash . . . . . . . . . . . 48

Cracked Wheat with Spinach and Pine Nuts . . . . . 49

Chickpeas with Peppers and Chard. . . . . . . . . . . 50

Pasta and Broccoli au Gratin . . . . . . . . . . . . . . 51

# Brussels Sprout and Celery Root Salad

People rarely use Brussels sprouts raw, which seems a shame as they have a very delicate flavor. This is a filling salad.

| | | |
|---|---|---|
| 1 cup | Brussels sprouts, trimmed and finely sliced | 250 mL |
| ½ cup | coarsely grated peeled celery root | 125 mL |
| | Juice of 1 lemon, divided | |
| 1 tsp | grated or prepared horseradish | 5 mL |
| 1 tbsp | light mayonnaise | 15 mL |
| | Freshly ground black pepper | |
| 1 to 2 tbsp | boiling water | 15 to 30 mL |
| 1 cup | arugula or lamb's lettuce | 250 mL |

1. In a large bowl, mix the Brussels sprouts with the celery root. Sprinkle with half of the lemon juice.

2. In a small bowl, mix the horseradish with the mayonnaise. Season with pepper to taste, then thin with boiling water to desired consistency.

3. Pour dressing over salad and toss to coat. Taste and add more pepper and lemon juice, if desired.

4. Just before serving, toss in the arugula.

## NUTRIENTS PER SERVING

| | |
|---|---|
| Calories | 130 |
| Carbohydrate | 24 g |
| Fiber | 5 g |
| Protein | 5 g |
| Fat | 3 g |
| Saturated fat | 1 g |
| Cholesterol | 4 mg |
| Sodium | 249 mg |

### Food Choices

| | |
|---|---|
| ½ | Fat |
| 1 | Extra |

# Cauliflower and Cashew Salad

**Makes 2 servings**

This very simple salad is both delicious and sustaining.

## Tip

All nuts, including cashews, have a very low glycemic load. Although they are high in calories, they are very nutritious, so they are worth enjoying in small amounts.

- **Steamer basket**

| | | |
|---|---|---|
| 1/2 | cauliflower, broken into florets | 1/2 |
| 2 tbsp | roasted salted cashews | 30 mL |
| 1 tbsp | olive oil | 15 mL |
| | Juice of 1/2 to 1 lemon | |
| | Freshly ground black pepper | |
| 4 | sprigs fresh parsley, chopped | 4 |

1. In a steamer basket set over a pot of simmering water, steam the cauliflower florets for 5 to 10 minutes or until they are just tender without being mushy.

2. Pour cauliflower into a bowl and mix in the cashews. Sprinkle with the oil and lemon juice to taste. Season with pepper. Sprinkle with parsley and serve warm or at room temperature.

## NUTRIENTS PER SERVING

| | |
|---|---|
| Calories | 148 |
| Carbohydrate | 12 g |
| Fiber | 4 g |
| Protein | 4 g |
| Fat | 11 g |
| Saturated fat | 2 g |
| Cholesterol | 0 mg |
| Sodium | 74 mg |

### Food Choices

| | |
|---|---|
| 2 | Fat |
| 1/2 | Extra |

# Spinach, Avocado and Mozzarella Salad

**Makes 2 servings**

This simple but delicious salad is perfect for lunch.

## Tip

Because this recipe is high in fat, it should be a special occasion treat on days when your fat consumption at other meals is low.

| | | |
|---|---|---|
| 2 cups | spinach leaves | 500 mL |
| ¼ | bulb fennel, thinly sliced | ¼ |
| ½ | young leek (white and light green part only), thinly sliced | ½ |
| ½ cup | alfalfa sprouts or other sprouted seeds | 125 mL |
| ½ | ripe avocado | ½ |
| 2 oz | bocconcini (about three 1-inch/2.5 cm balls) or buffalo mozzarella | 60 g |
| 1 tbsp | pine nuts | 15 mL |
| 2 to 3 | sprigs fresh basil, some leaves chopped | 2 to 3 |
| Pinch | sea salt | Pinch |
| | Freshly ground black pepper | |
| | Juice of 1 lemon | |
| 1 tbsp | extra virgin olive oil | 15 mL |

1. Tear up the spinach leaves and arrange them in the bottom of a serving dish. Sprinkle with the fennel, leek and sprouts.

2. Peel the avocado and slice it lengthwise. Arrange avocado slices over the leaves.

3. Slice the mozzarella and lay it out in the middle of the dish. Sprinkle with the pine nuts, then decorate with basil leaves, both chopped and whole. Season with a pinch of salt and with pepper to taste, then drizzle with lemon juice and oil. Serve immediately.

## NUTRIENTS PER SERVING

| | |
|---|---|
| Calories | 292 |
| Carbohydrate | 13 g |
| Fiber | 5 g |
| Protein | 6 g |
| Fat | 24 g |
| Saturated fat | 7 g |
| Cholesterol | 25 mg |
| Sodium | 137 mg |

### Food Choices

| | |
|---|---|
| ½ | Meat & Alternatives |
| 4½ | Fat |
| ½ | Extra |

# Avocados and Sprouts

Avocados have a negligible glycemic load but tons of vitamin C (among other worthwhile nutrients), and are both easily digestible and delicious. Sprouts provide vitamin C, vitamin K, riboflavin, folate, magnesium, phosphorus, zinc, copper, manganese, protein, vitamin A, thiamin, pantothenic acid, calcium and iron. Combine the two, as with the Spinach, Avocado and Mozzarella Salad (opposite), and you'll feel like a new person!

# Fennel and Strawberry Salad

The arrival of fresh local strawberries is always worth celebrating, so here is a slightly unusual but delicious salad for early summer.

## Tip

If you are concerned about pesticide residues, strawberries are one fruit you should always buy organic. Conventionally grown strawberries are sprayed not just once, but throughout their growing season.

| | | |
|---|---|---|
| ½ | bulb fennel | ½ |
| 1 tbsp | plain yogurt (cow's, sheep's, goat's or soy) | 15 mL |
| | Juice of ¼ to ½ lemon | |
| 2 to 3 | fresh mint leaves, chopped | 2 to 3 |
| 4 to 5 | strawberries, halved or quartered depending on their size | 4 to 5 |

1. Trim the fennel and slice it thinly, reserving a few fronds for garnish.

2. Blanch the sliced fennel in a pot of boiling water for 3 minutes. Plunge into a bowl of ice water, then drain.

3. Meanwhile, mix the yogurt with lemon juice to taste. Stir in mint gradually, tasting often (its flavor is very strong and can overwhelm the dressing if you're not cautious).

4. Toss the fennel and strawberries in the dressing and arrange on a serving dish. Decorate with the reserved fennel fronds.

### NUTRIENTS PER SERVING

| | |
|---|---|
| Calories | 46 |
| Carbohydrate | 10 g |
| Fiber | 3 g |
| Protein | 2 g |
| Fat | 1 g |
| Saturated fat | 0 g |
| Cholesterol | 2 mg |
| Sodium | 101 mg |

**Food Choices**

| | |
|---|---|
| ½ | Extra |

# Spaghetti and Pine Nut Salad

Use really nice fresh herbs in this simple, light summer pasta entrée — they make all the difference.

## Tip

Like all nuts, pine nuts are an excellent source of nutrients, especially vitamin E and zinc. They are also high in monounsaturated fats — good for blood sugar control!

| | | |
|---|---|---|
| 5 oz | spaghetti or other long pasta | 150 g |
| 1 tbsp | good-quality olive oil | 15 mL |
| 6 | green onions, trimmed and chopped | 6 |
| 2 | large handfuls of fresh parsley or cilantro (or a mixture), chopped | 2 |
| 2 tbsp | pine nuts or sunflower seeds | 30 mL |
| | Juice of 1 lemon | |
| Pinch | sea salt | Pinch |
| | Freshly ground black pepper | |

1. In a large pot of boiling water, cook the pasta according to the package instructions, omitting salt. When just al dente, remove from heat, drain, reserving $1/4$ cup (60 mL) of the cooking water, pour into a bowl and mix in the oil.

2. Allow the pasta to cool slightly, then mix in the green onions, parsley and pine nuts. Drizzle with the lemon juice and enough of the cooking water to moisten. Season with a pinch of salt and with pepper to taste.

## NUTRIENTS PER SERVING

| | |
|---|---|
| Calories | 422 |
| Carbohydrate | 63 g |
| Fiber | 6 g |
| Protein | 13 g |
| Fat | 14 g |
| Saturated fat | 2 g |
| Cholesterol | 0 mg |
| Sodium | 123 mg |

### Food Choices

| | |
|---|---|
| $3^1/2$ | Carbohydrate |
| $2^1/2$ | Fat |
| $1/2$ | Extra |

# Warm Pasta and Curly Kale Salad

**Makes 1 serving**

Pasta is often best served warm, rather than hot — which puts less pressure on the cook. In this filling entrée salad, the stronger flavor of whole-grain pasta is a good match for the curly kale.

• **Steamer basket**

| | | |
|---|---|---|
| 2 tsp | olive oil, divided | 10 mL |
| 1 | small onion, thinly sliced | 1 |
| 4 or 5 | small button mushrooms, halved or sliced | 4 or 5 |
| 2½ oz | whole-grain penne pasta | 75 g |
| 1 cup | chopped trimmed curly kale leaves | 250 mL |
| 2 tbsp | green pumpkin seeds (pepitas) or mixed seeds, lightly toasted | 30 mL |
| | Juice of ¼ lemon | |
| Pinch | sea salt | Pinch |
| | Freshly ground black pepper | |

1. In a small pan, heat half of the oil over medium heat. Cook the onion, stirring often, for 5 to 8 minutes or until quite soft.

2. Add the mushrooms, increase the heat and cook for 2 to 3 minutes or until the mushrooms start to give their juice.

3. Meanwhile, in a large pot of boiling water, cook the pasta according to the package instructions, omitting salt. Drain and set aside.

4. In a steamer basket set over a saucepan of simmering water, steam the kale for 2 minutes or until lightly cooked but still green and a little crunchy.

5. In a large serving dish, toss the onion mixture with the pasta. Add the steamed kale and the seeds. Drizzle with the remaining oil and lemon juice. Season with a pinch of salt and with pepper to taste. Serve warm or at room temperature.

## NUTRIENTS PER SERVING

| Calories | 472 |
|---|---|
| Carbohydrate | 67 g |
| Fiber | 9 g |
| Protein | 18 g |
| Fat | 19 g |
| Saturated fat | 3 g |
| Cholesterol | 0 mg |
| Sodium | 201 mg |

### Food Choices

| 3 | Carbohydrate |
|---|---|
| ½ | Meat & Alternatives |
| 3 | Fat |

# Seeds

Seeds of all kinds — pumpkin, sunflower, sesame — are both delicious and highly nutritious. Like nuts, their flavor is really released by roasting or toasting. It only takes a minute and is well worth the effort. If you use salted seeds in a recipe, you likely won't need any added salt.

# Beet and Chickpea Salad

Chickpeas and butter beans work equally well in this salad, so take your pick. The salad benefits from time to mature, so if you have too much it will be fine for at least 24 hours in the fridge.

## Tip

To prepare this salad on the stovetop instead of in the microwave, combine the ingredients in a small saucepan. Warm over medium-low heat for 2 to 3 minutes, then transfer to a dish to stand for 2 to 3 hours.

| | | |
|---|---|---|
| 1 | beet, peeled and grated | 1 |
| 1 | can (14 oz/398 mL) chickpeas or butter beans, drained and rinsed | 1 |
| 3 | green onions, trimmed and chopped | 3 |
| 1 tbsp | reduced-sodium soy sauce | 15 mL |
| 1 tbsp | vinegar (of your choice) | 15 mL |
| 1 tbsp | olive oil (or 1½ tsp/7 mL each olive and pumpkin oil) | 15 mL |
| | Freshly ground black pepper | |

1. In a microwave-safe dish with a cover, mix the grated beet with the chickpeas and green onions. Add the soy sauce, vinegar, oil and pepper to taste, and mix again thoroughly.

2. Cover the dish and microwave on High for 1 minute (this helps the chickpeas and beet absorb the dressing).

3. Let stand at room temperature for 2 to 3 hours (do not chill). Mix again thoroughly before serving.

## NUTRIENTS PER SERVING

| | |
|---|---|
| Calories | 237 |
| Carbohydrate | 31 g |
| Fiber | 8 g |
| Protein | 10 g |
| Fat | 9 g |
| Saturated fat | 1 g |
| Cholesterol | 0 mg |
| Sodium | 319 mg |

### Food Choices

| | |
|---|---|
| 1 | Carbohydrate |
| 1 | Meat & Alternatives |
| 1 | Fat |

# Chicken and Apple Salad

This recipe is based on one from a cookbook by Joan Cromwell (wife of Oliver). She decorated the salad with the bones of the chicken, but you don't need to recreate the recipe to that extent! The combination is delicious.

| | | |
|---|---|---|
| 3 oz | cooked boneless skinless chicken, cut into strips | 90 g |
| 2 to 3 | sprigs of fresh parsley or watercress, roughly chopped | 2 to 3 |
| 1 | shallot (or ½ small onion), finely chopped | 1 |
| ½ | small tart eating apple (unpeeled), cut into small dice | ½ |
| | Watercress or lettuce leaves | |
| | Grated zest and juice of ½ to 1 lemon | |
| Pinch | sea salt | Pinch |
| | Freshly ground black pepper | |
| 1 tbsp | olive oil | 15 mL |

1. In a bowl, mix the chicken, parsley, shallot, apple, watercress and lemon zest to taste. Season with a pinch of salt and with pepper to taste. Drizzle with olive oil and lemon juice to taste. Mix well.

2. Serve over extra watercress leaves.

## NUTRIENTS PER SERVING

| | |
|---|---|
| Calories | 316 |
| Carbohydrate | 16 g |
| Fiber | 3 g |
| Protein | 27 g |
| Fat | 16 g |
| Saturated fat | 3 g |
| Cholesterol | 70 mg |
| Sodium | 218 mg |

### Food Choices

| | |
|---|---|
| ½ | Carbohydrate |
| 3½ | Meat & Alternatives |
| 1 | Fat |

# Pepper, Pear and Anchovy Salad

Here's a delicious, cool and refreshing salad for a hot summer day. Save the second pear half to have with a slice of blue cheese for dessert.

## Tip

There's no need to add salt to the dressing, as the saltiness of the anchovies will develop in the mayonnaise.

| | | |
|---|---|---|
| 1 tbsp | light mayonnaise | 15 mL |
| 1 to 2 | drained canned anchovy fillets, finely chopped | 1 to 2 |
| | Freshly ground black pepper | |
| | Lemon juice | |
| | Boiling water (optional) | |
| ½ | red bell pepper, thinly sliced | ½ |
| ½ | pear, peeled and thinly sliced | ½ |
| 3 to 4 | crisp lettuce leaves (such as iceberg or romaine) | 3 to 4 |

1. Put the mayonnaise in a bowl, then add the anchovy. Mix well, then season with pepper and lemon juice to taste. The mayonnaise should be of a light coating consistency, like whipping cream; if it is too thick, thin it with a little boiling water.

2. Add the red pepper and pear and toss gently until well coated with dressing.

3. Serve on a bed of lettuce.

| NUTRIENTS PER SERVING | |
|---|---|
| Calories | 124 |
| Carbohydrate | 21 g |
| Fiber | 4 g |
| Protein | 2 g |
| Fat | 4 g |
| Saturated fat | 0 g |
| Cholesterol | 7 mg |
| Sodium | 274 mg |
| **Food Choices** | |
| ½ | Carbohydrate |
| ½ | Extra |

# Anchovies

Keeping a small tin of anchovies on hand can be very useful. Because anchovies are salty and packed in oil, they keep for ages, and they are a great way of adding seasoning to a recipe if you do not want to use too much salt. They work just as well in meat dishes as they do in fish dishes.

# Fresh Seafood Salad

Many supermarkets sell ready-cooked mixtures of shrimp, mussels, squid and other seafood, so this a very quick and easy dish to prepare. Alternatively, buy 3 oz (90 g) per person of any combination of seafood; simmer it gently in fish stock or in lightly seasoned water mixed with a little white wine. Serve with a new potato salad or a green salad.

| | | |
|---|---|---|
| 3 oz | mixed cooked seafood (thawed and drained if frozen) | 90 g |
| 4 | small green onions, trimmed and finely chopped | 4 |
| 2 | tomatoes, peeled, seeded and chopped | 2 |
| 1 | small bulb fennel, trimmed and very thinly sliced | 1 |
| ¼ | small mild red chile pepper (or a generous pinch of cayenne pepper) | ¼ |
| 1 tsp | olive oil | 5 mL |
| | Juice of 1 lemon | |
| | Freshly ground black pepper | |

1. In a bowl, combine seafood, green onions, tomatoes, fennel, chile pepper, oil and lemon juice to taste. Season with pepper to taste.

2. Cover and refrigerate for at least 15 minutes or up to 1 hour before serving.

## NUTRIENTS PER SERVING

| | |
|---|---|
| Calories | 288 |
| Carbohydrate | 24 g |
| Fiber | 6 g |
| Protein | 34 g |
| Fat | 9 g |
| Saturated fat | 1 g |
| Cholesterol | 129 mg |
| Sodium | 487 mg |

### Food Choices

| | |
|---|---|
| ½ | Carbohydrate |
| 4 | Meat & Alternatives |
| 1 | Extra |

Watercress Soup (page 14)

Carrot and Red Lentil Soup (page 15)

Ajwar (page 22)

Eggs au Miroir (page 23)

Brussels Sprout and Celery Root Salad (page 28)

Fennel and Strawberry Salad (page 32)

Beet and Chickpea Salad (page 36)

Chicken Salad with Pumpkin Oil (page 42)

Cracked Wheat with Spinach
and Pine Nuts (page 49)

Pasta and Broccoli au Gratin (page 51)

Fusilli with Capers and Anchovies (page 54)

# Chile Peppers

Some studies show that chile peppers have a beneficial effect on blood sugar control. In addition, they help control pain and aid in clearing the nose and lungs of congestion. They also contain significant amounts of vitamin A, vitamin C, calcium, iron and potassium.

# Chicken Salad with Pumpkin Oil

The pumpkin oil and balsamic vinegar combine to make a really delicious dressing for the chicken. If you treated yourself to a roast chicken and have lots of meat over, this would be a great way to use it up. Serve with new potatoes and a cucumber salad.

| | | |
|---|---|---|
| 2 tsp | olive oil | 10 mL |
| 1 | onion, very thinly sliced | 1 |
| 6 oz | cooked boneless skinless chicken breast and/or thigh meat | 175 g |
| Pinch | sea salt | Pinch |
| | Freshly ground black pepper | |
| 1 tbsp | toasted pumpkin seed oil | 15 mL |
| 1 tbsp | balsamic vinegar | 15 mL |
| | Baby spinach | |
| | Red or white Belgian endive leaves | |
| | Nasturtium flowers to decorate (optional) | |

1. In a heavy, wide pan, heat the oil over low heat. Add the sliced onion and stir thoroughly so that the onion is well broken up. Cook, stirring occasionally, for 30 minutes. The onion should very gradually change color and dry out, but must not burn. Add a little water to prevent burning as necessary as the onion caramelizes.

2. Slice the chicken meat and season with a pinch of salt and with pepper to taste. Place half the meat in a bowl. Sprinkle with one-third of the onion.

3. In a separate bowl, mix the pumpkin oil and balsamic vinegar. Spoon half of this dressing over the chicken mixture in the bowl.

4. Place another layer of chicken in the bowl, followed by another one-third of the onion and the remaining dressing. Place the remaining onion in a small bowl. Cover both the salad and the onion, and refrigerate both for 3 to 4 hours to allow the salad to marinate.

5. To serve, arrange the spinach and endive on two plates. Arrange the chicken mixture on top. If there is any dressing left in the bowl, drizzle it over the chicken. Sprinkle with the reserved onion.

## NUTRIENTS PER SERVING

| | |
|---|---|
| Calories | 263 |
| Carbohydrate | 4 g |
| Fiber | 0 g |
| Protein | 27 g |
| Fat | 15 g |
| Saturated fat | 3 g |
| Cholesterol | 74 mg |
| Sodium | 145 mg |

### Food Choices

| | |
|---|---|
| 4 | Meat & Alternatives |
| 1/2 | Fat |

# Balsamic Vinegar

Balsamic vinegar has become all the rage over the last few years. As a result, much of what is on sale is of inferior quality and is often sweetened with sugar. Real balsamic vinegar is slightly sweet, but the sweetness derives from the long aging of the grape pressings in different wooden kegs — chestnut, cherry, ash, mulberry and juniper. It is rich and complex in flavor. For people with diabetes, it should be used very sparingly in a dish that is low in both fat and carbohydrate.

# Red Cabbage Casserole

This great winter casserole can be enjoyed either as a side dish or a light meal. It is easy to make, filling, flavorsome, low-GI and nutritious. It also reheats well, so it is worth making enough for two meals even if you are on your own.

## Tip

Yogurt goes really well with red cabbage, so you might like to finish off the dish with a spoonful of plain yogurt on the top of each portion before you serve it.

### NUTRIENTS PER SERVING

| | |
|---|---|
| Calories | 283 |
| Carbohydrate | 42 g |
| Fiber | 8 g |
| Protein | 6 g |
| Fat | 12 g |
| Saturated fat | 1 g |
| Cholesterol | 0 mg |
| Sodium | 156 mg |

### Food Choices

| | |
|---|---|
| 1 | Carbohydrate |
| 2½ | Fat |
| 1 | Extra |

• **Heavy casserole dish**

| | | |
|---|---|---|
| 1 tbsp | sunflower or olive oil | 15 mL |
| 1 | large onion, sliced | 1 |
| ⅓ | red cabbage, fairly thinly sliced | ⅓ |
| 2 | small sweet potatoes, peeled and diced | 2 |
| 1 | small tart cooking apple, peeled and diced | 1 |
| 1 tsp | dried dillweed | 5 mL |
| Pinch | ground nutmeg (or freshly grated, if possible) | Pinch |
| ½ tsp | coriander seeds | 2 mL |
| 6 tbsp | water or no-salt-added ready-to-use vegetable broth | 90 mL |
| 1 tbsp | green pumpkin seeds (pepitas) | 15 mL |
| 1 tbsp | unsalted sunflower seeds | 15 mL |
| | Juice of ½ large lemon | |
| Pinch | sea salt | Pinch |
| | Freshly ground black pepper | |

1. In a heavy casserole dish, heat the oil over medium heat. Add the onion, cabbage, sweet potatoes, apple, dill, nutmeg, coriander seeds and water. Bring to a simmer, then reduce heat to low, cover and simmer for 30 minutes or until the sweet potato is tender and the red cabbage is cooked but still retains some crunch.

2. Stir in the pumpkin seeds, sunflower seeds and lemon juice. Season with a pinch of salt and with pepper to taste.

# Kale with Beet Leaves

**Makes 2 servings**

This is a seriously nutritious side dish — even more so if you can find fresh beets that are still attached to their stalks and leaves, as the leaves are even more laden with nutrients than the beets themselves. Use the beets for the Beet and Chickpea Salad on page 36. If you have leftovers, they work well as a salad, especially with something relatively bland like a hard- or soft-cooked egg.

| | | |
|---|---|---|
| 1 tbsp | olive oil | 15 mL |
| 1 | small onion, sliced | 1 |
| ½ | large tart cooking apple (unpeeled), finely chopped | ½ |
| Pinch | sea salt | Pinch |
| 6 cups | trimmed curly kale (9 oz/270 g), coarsely chopped | 1.5 L |
| 1 cup | beet greens with stalks (or extra kale), coarsely chopped | 250 mL |
| 1 to 2 tbsp | water (optional) | 15 to 30 mL |
| | Freshly ground black pepper | |

1. In a deep pan, heat the oil over medium heat. Cook the onion, apple and salt, stirring often, for 5 to 8 minutes or until the onion is quite soft (but watch it carefully as it can burn very easily).

2. Add kale and beet greens, reduce heat to medium-low, cover and cook, stirring often, for 5 to 10 minutes or until the greens are cooked but retain a little crunch. If they appear to be drying up, add a little water — the mixture should be moist without being wet.

3. Season with pepper to taste before serving.

### NUTRIENTS PER SERVING

| | |
|---|---|
| Calories | 165 |
| Carbohydrate | 22 g |
| Fiber | 5 g |
| Protein | 7 g |
| Fat | 8 g |
| Saturated fat | 1 g |
| Cholesterol | 0 mg |
| Sodium | 174 mg |

**Food Choices**

| | |
|---|---|
| 1½ | Fat |
| 1 | Extra |

# Celery Root with Kale and Pecans

**Makes 1 serving**

This dish can be served as a side dish with a roast or as a vegetarian meal on its own. The contrast between the pale celery root and the dark kale is both beautiful and flavorful.

- **Steamer basket**
- **Food processor**

| | | |
|---|---|---|
| ½ | small celery root | ½ |
| 1 tsp | butter (or 1 tbsp/15 mL goat, soy or oat cream) | 5 mL |
| Pinch | ground nutmeg | Pinch |
| | Freshly ground black pepper | |
| 3 cups | packed trimmed curly kale leaves, chopped | 750 mL |
| 1 tbsp | toasted chopped pecans | 15 mL |

1. Trim the celery root and cut into cubes. Place in a steamer basket over a saucepan of simmering water and steam until tender.

2. Transfer the celery root to the food processor and purée with the butter or cream until smooth. Season with a pinch of nutmeg and with pepper to taste.

3. Place the kale in the steamer basket over a saucepan of simmering water. Steam until just cooked. Mix the kale into the puréed celery root mixture.

4. Turn onto a warmed serving plate and sprinkle with the toasted pecans.

## NUTRIENTS PER SERVING

| | |
|---|---|
| Calories | 222 |
| Carbohydrate | 26 g |
| Fiber | 6 g |
| Protein | 11 g |
| Fat | 12 g |
| Saturated fat | 3 g |
| Cholesterol | 11 mg |
| Sodium | 190 mg |

### Food Choices

| | |
|---|---|
| 2 | Fat |
| 1 | Extra |

# Pecans

Pecans are another really delicious food that is "free" on the glycemic index and filled with nutrition. Often used as an alternative to walnuts, they actually have a sweeter, smoother flavor that is really accentuated by roasting or toasting.

# Ratatouille with Butternut Squash

Adding butternut squash to ratatouille gives it added dimension in both flavor and texture. This dish keeps really well if you have some left over.

## Tip

Squashes are not the lowest vegetables on the glycemic tables, but in this dish they are combined with vegetables that do not appear on the tables at all; as a result, the overall profile of the dish is very acceptable.

### NUTRIENTS PER SERVING

| | |
|---|---|
| Calories | 211 |
| Carbohydrate | 35 g |
| Fiber | 8 g |
| Protein | 6 g |
| Fat | 8 g |
| Saturated fat | 1 g |
| Cholesterol | 0 mg |
| Sodium | 108 mg |

#### Food Choices

| | |
|---|---|
| 1 | Carbohydrate |
| 1 | Fat |
| 1 | Extra |

**Preheat broiler (optional)**

| | | |
|---|---|---|
| 1 tbsp | olive oil | 15 mL |
| 1 | small onion, sliced | 1 |
| 1 | small red bell pepper, thinly sliced | 1 |
| 1 | small yellow bell pepper, thinly sliced | 1 |
| 2 | medium-large zucchini, sliced | 2 |
| 1 | small butternut squash, peeled and diced | 1 |
| 1½ tsp | dried oregano or herbes de Provence | 7 mL |
| 8 | cherry tomatoes, halved | 8 |
| Pinch | sea salt | Pinch |
| | Freshly ground black pepper | |
| ¼ cup | shredded Cheddar cheese or freshly grated Parmesan cheese (optional) | 60 mL |

1. In a heavy pan, heat the oil over medium heat. Cook the onion, red pepper and yellow pepper, stirring often, for 5 to 10 minutes or until starting to soften.

2. Add the zucchini, squash and oregano. Increase heat slightly and cook, stirring often, for 5 minutes.

3. Stir in the tomatoes and season with a pinch of salt and with pepper to taste. Reduce heat to medium-low, cover and cook gently for 15 to 20 minutes or until the zucchini and squash are tender.

4. Remove the lid and, if there is too much liquid, continue to cook gently, uncovered, for 5 minutes.

5. Transfer the ratatouille to a warmed dish (ovenproof if you'll be using the broiler). If using cheese, sprinkle it on top of the ratatouille and place under the preheated broiler for a few minutes, until cheese is browned but not burned.

# Cracked Wheat with Spinach and Pine Nuts

**Makes 2 servings**

This recipe is inspired by one from an ancient Roman cookbook and is an unusual and tasty combination.

## Tip

While cracked wheat is not particularly low on the glycemic index, it is not high either, so it is fine when combined with very low-GI foods, such as the other vegetables — and especially okra, whose mucilaginous texture helps, with blood sugar control.

| NUTRIENTS PER SERVING | |
|---|---|
| Calories | 280 |
| Carbohydrate | 34 g |
| Fiber | 6 g |
| Protein | 6 g |
| Fat | 13 g |
| Saturated fat | 2 g |
| Cholesterol | 0 mg |
| Sodium | 114 mg |
| **Food Choices** | |
| 1½ | Carbohydrate |
| 2½ | Fat |
| ½ | Extra |

- **Steamer basket**

| 1 tbsp | olive oil | 15 mL |
|---|---|---|
| 2 oz | okra, trimmed and cut into rounds | 60 g |
| ¼ tsp | ground cumin | 1 mL |
| ¾ cup | button mushrooms, sliced | 175 mL |
| 2 cups | packed spinach, trimmed and chopped | 500 mL |
| ¼ cup | cracked wheat or bulgur | 60 mL |
| 3 to 7 tbsp | boiling water | 45 to 105 mL |
| ¼ cup | dry white wine (or 1 tbsp/15 mL white wine vinegar) | 60 mL |
| ¼ cup | raisins | 60 mL |
| ½ cup | snow peas, cut in half | 125 mL |
| 2 tbsp | pine nuts | 30 mL |
| | Juice of ¼ to ½ lemon | |
| Pinch | sea salt | Pinch |
| | Freshly ground black pepper | |

1. In a large saucepan, heat the oil over medium heat. Cook the okra and cumin, stirring often, for 2 minutes. Add the mushrooms and spinach, and cook, stirring, for 2 to 3 minutes, until both are somewhat wilted.

2. Meanwhile, place the cracked wheat in a bowl and spoon the boiling water over top. Leave to swell for about 5 minutes.

3. In a steamer basket over a saucepan of simmering water, lightly steam the snow peas so that they are partially cooked but still crunchy.

4. Add the cracked wheat and raisins to the okra mixture and cook for 2 to 3 minutes or until heated through. Stir in the snow peas and pine nuts. Drizzle with lemon juice to taste. Season with a pinch of salt and with pepper to taste. Serve immediately.

# Chickpeas with Peppers and Chard

Chickpeas are a good carb choice for people with diabetes, as they are very high in fiber and low on the glycemic index.

## Tip

Look for a vegetable broth with less than 20 g of sodium per $\frac{2}{3}$ cup (150 mL), or make your own with no added salt.

| | | |
|---|---|---|
| 1 tbsp | olive oil, divided | 15 mL |
| 1 | red bell pepper, cut into long strips | 1 |
| 2 tbsp | minced gingerroot | 30 mL |
| 1 tsp | cumin powder | 5 mL |
| 2 | cloves garlic, thinly sliced | 2 |
| 2 cups | chopped trimmed Swiss chard or other dark mixed greens | 500 mL |
| $\frac{1}{2}$ cup | drained rinsed canned chickpeas | 125 mL |
| $\frac{1}{4}$ cup | no-salt-added or reduced-sodium ready-to-use vegetable broth | 60 mL |
| | Freshly ground black pepper | |

1. In a frying pan, heat half of the oil over medium-low heat. Add the red pepper and cook, stirring occasionally, for 20 minutes or until quite soft.

2. Meanwhile, in a heavy pan, heat the remaining oil over medium-low heat. Add the ginger, cumin and garlic and cook, stirring often, for about 3 minutes or until the garlic has softened (be careful not to burn it).

3. Add the Swiss chard, chickpeas and broth to the ginger mixture. Increase heat and bring to a boil, then reduce heat to medium-low, cover and simmer for 7 to 12 minutes (depending on the type of greens you use) or until greens are tender and chickpeas have absorbed the flavor of the vegetables.

4. Stir the cooked red peppers and their oil into the chickpea mixture. Season with pepper to taste.

5. Remove from heat and let cool to room temperature before serving.

## NUTRIENTS PER SERVING

| | |
|---|---|
| Calories | 290 |
| Carbohydrate | 31 g |
| Fiber | 8 g |
| Protein | 8 g |
| Fat | 16 g |
| Saturated fat | 2 g |
| Cholesterol | 0 mg |
| Sodium | 182 mg |

### Food Choices

| | |
|---|---|
| $\frac{1}{2}$ | Carbohydrate |
| $\frac{1}{2}$ | Meat & Alternatives |
| $2\frac{1}{2}$ | Fat |
| 1 | Extra |

# Pasta and Broccoli au Gratin

A classic with a twist, this cheesy pasta dish is hearty enough for a main course.

## Tip

Because this recipe is high in fat, it should be a special occasion treat on days when your fat consumption at other meals is low.

### NUTRIENTS PER SERVING

| | |
|---|---|
| Calories | 590 |
| Carbohydrate | 66 g |
| Fiber | 10 g |
| Protein | 20 g |
| Fat | 26 g |
| Saturated fat | 15 g |
| Cholesterol | 69 mg |
| Sodium | 427 mg |

### Food Choices

| | |
|---|---|
| 3 | Carbohydrate |
| 1½ | Meat & Alternatives |
| 3 | Fat |
| 1 | Extra |

**• Preheat broiler**

| | | |
|---|---|---|
| 2 oz | whole-grain penne or fusilli pasta | 60 g |
| 1 cup | broccoli or cauliflower florets, or a mixture of the two | 250 mL |
| ½ | small onion, coarsely chopped | ½ |
| 1 tbsp | butter or olive oil | 15 mL |
| 1 tbsp | all-purpose flour | 15 mL |
| 6 tbsp | milk (cow's, soy or oat milk) | 90 mL |
| 2 tbsp | dry white wine (or 2 tsp/10 mL white wine vinegar) | 30 mL |
| ¼ cup | shredded sharp (old) Cheddar cheese, divided | 60 mL |
| 1 tsp | whole-grain or Dijon mustard | 5 mL |
| | Sea salt and freshly ground black pepper | |

1. In a large pot of boiling water, cook the pasta according to the package instructions, omitting salt. Drain and keep warm, reserving a little of the water to thin the sauce if needed.

2. Meanwhile, steam the broccoli and/or cauliflower and onion until just cooked but still slightly al dente.

3. While the pasta and vegetables are cooking, melt the butter in a pan over medium heat. Stir in the flour. Cook, stirring, for 1 minute, then slowly add the milk. Heat, stirring constantly, until the sauce thickens. Do not let boil. Add three-quarters of the cheese, stirring until melted. Stir in the mustard. Season with salt and pepper to taste. If the sauce is too thick, thin it with a little of the pasta water.

4. Gently mix the pasta with the vegetables and sauce, then spoon into a warmed casserole or pie dish. Sprinkle the remaining cheese over the top and brown under the preheated broiler. Serve immediately.

# Fish and Seafood

Fusilli with Capers and Anchovies . . . . . . . . . . . . 54

Fish Fillets with Curly Kale . . . . . . . . . . . . . . . . . . 55

Haddock Pie . . . . . . . . . . . . . . . . . . . . . . . . . . 56

Cod with Clams and Coconut Milk . . . . . . . . . . . 58

Fillet of Cod with Chiles . . . . . . . . . . . . . . . . . . . 60

Salmon Steamed with Fennel and Tomatoes . . . . . 61

Salmon with Asian Greens . . . . . . . . . . . . . . . . . 62

Fettuccine with Smoked Salmon
  and Cream Sauce . . . . . . . . . . . . . . . . . . . . . 63

Baked Trout with Apple . . . . . . . . . . . . . . . . . . . 64

Poached Trout with Rhubarb Sauce . . . . . . . . . . . 65

Tuna with Beets and Red Cabbage . . . . . . . . . . . 66

Stir-Fried Tuna with Snow Peas . . . . . . . . . . . . . . 68

Moules Marinières . . . . . . . . . . . . . . . . . . . . . . . 69

Stir-Fried Shrimp with Ginger . . . . . . . . . . . . . . . 70

New Orleans Jambalaya . . . . . . . . . . . . . . . . . . . 71

# Fusilli with Capers and Anchovies

The capers and anchovies give this recipe a hearty, Italian country cooking flavor. The sauce works better if you cook more of it, so I have given the recipe for two. Any excess will keep for several days in the fridge. Serve with a green salad.

## Tip

The glycemic load of pasta is lower if you cook it until al dente, with just a tiny bit of chewiness.

| NUTRIENTS PER SERVING | |
|---|---|
| Calories | 339 |
| Carbohydrate | 55 g |
| Fiber | 1 g |
| Protein | 13 g |
| Fat | 8 g |
| Saturated fat | 1 g |
| Cholesterol | 3 mg |
| Sodium | 192 mg |
| **Food Choices** | |
| 3 Carbohydrate | |
| 1 Fat | |

| | | |
|---|---|---|
| 5 oz | whole-grain fusilli or other short pasta | 150 g |
| 1 tbsp | olive oil | 15 mL |
| 2 | drained canned anchovy fillets, finely chopped | 2 |
| 2 | shallots, chopped | 2 |
| 2 | cloves garlic, sliced | 2 |
| 5 | mushrooms, coarsely chopped | 5 |
| 1 tsp | drained capers, chopped | 5 mL |
| ¼ cup | dry white wine (or 1 tbsp/15 mL white wine vinegar) | 60 mL |
| 2 | sprigs fresh parsley, trimmed and chopped | 2 |
| | Freshly ground black pepper | |

1. In a pot of boiling water, cook the fusilli according to the package instructions, omitting salt. Drain the fusilli, reserving a little of the cooking water.

2. Meanwhile, in a small pan, heat the olive oil over medium heat. Cook the anchovies, shallots and garlic, stirring often, for 4 to 5 minutes.

3. Add the mushrooms, increase the heat and cook for 2 to 3 minutes or until the mushrooms start to give their juice.

4. Add the capers and wine, and cook for 2 minutes. Add the parsley and enough cooking water to make the sauce the consistency of cream. Season with pepper to taste.

5. Mix the sauce gently into the fusilli. Serve immediately.

# Fish Fillets with Curly Kale

**Makes 1 serving**

Sea vegetables, seaweed and seaweed condiments work particularly well with fish, kale and parsnips. They are also extremely nutritious (one of the best sources of iodine) as well as tasty — much better than salt.

- **Steamer basket**

| | | |
|---|---|---|
| 1 | medium parsnip (or 2 small), thickly sliced | 1 |
| 1 tsp | olive oil | 5 mL |
| 1 | onion, thickly sliced | 1 |
| 2 cups | packed shredded trimmed curly kale | 500 mL |
| 1½ tsp | crumbled dried sea vegetables or Japanese seaweed | 7 mL |
| 3 oz | skinless firm white fish fillet, such as halibut, haddock or striped bass | 90 g |
| Pinch | sea salt | Pinch |
| | Freshly ground black pepper | |
| 3 to 4 tbsp | water, a mix of water and white wine, or unsalted fish stock | 45 to 60 mL |
| ½ | lemon | ½ |

1. In a steamer basket set over a pot of simmering water, steam the sliced parsnips for 8 to 10 minutes or until almost tender.

2. Meanwhile, in a large saucepan, heat the oil over medium heat. Cook the onion for 4 to 5 minutes, stirring often, or until it is starting to soften.

3. Add the steamed parsnips, kale and sea vegetables, stirring gently. Place the fish on top and season lightly with salt and pepper. Pour the water around the fish. Cover, reduce heat to low and cook for about 15 minutes or until the kale is cooked and the fish is opaque and flakes easily when tested with a fork.

4. Serve from the pan, with a squeeze of lemon.

## NUTRIENTS PER SERVING

| | |
|---|---|
| Calories | 284 |
| Carbohydrate | 36 g |
| Fiber | 7 g |
| Protein | 24 g |
| Fat | 7 g |
| Saturated fat | 1 g |
| Cholesterol | 42 mg |
| Sodium | 282 mg |

### Food Choices

| | |
|---|---|
| 2 | Meat & Alternatives |
| 1 | Extra |

# Haddock Pie

**Makes 2 servings**

A pie with a difference: the potatoes are at the bottom rather than on top. If you are on your own, it will reheat well for a second meal.

- **Preheat oven to 350°F (180°C)**
- **Steamer basket**
- **Pie dish**

| 2 | potatoes, thickly sliced | 2 |
|---|---|---|
| 1 tbsp | olive oil | 15 mL |
| 2 | leeks (white and light green parts only), thickly sliced | 2 |
| 2 | zucchini, thickly sliced | 2 |
| 1½ tsp | dried oregano | 7 mL |
| 1 | can (14 oz/398 mL) diced tomatoes (or 1½ cups/375 mL) | 1 |
| 6 oz | skinless haddock or other firm white fish fillets | 175 g |
| Pinch | sea salt | Pinch |
| | Freshly ground black pepper | |
| 1 tbsp | mixed unsalted green pumpkin seeds (pepitas) and sunflower seeds | 15 mL |

1. In a steamer basket set over a saucepan of simmering water, steam the potatoes until tender.

2. Meanwhile, in a wide pan, heat the oil over medium-low heat. Cook the leeks, stirring often, for 5 minutes.

3. Add the zucchini and oregano, increase the heat to medium and cook for 5 to 10 minutes or until leeks and zucchini are lightly browned.

4. Add the tomatoes and cook for 2 to 3 minutes to combine the flavors.

5. Arrange the potato slices in the bottom of the pie dish. Lay the haddock on top of the potatoes and season with salt and pepper. Spoon the vegetables over the fish.

## NUTRIENTS PER SERVING

| | |
|---|---|
| Calories | 457 |
| Carbohydrate | 74 g |
| Fiber | 9 g |
| Protein | 25 g |
| Fat | 10 g |
| Saturated fat | 1 g |
| Cholesterol | 46 mg |
| Sodium | 312 mg |

### Food Choices

| 3 | Carbohydrate |
|---|---|
| 2½ | Meat & Alternatives |
| 1 | Extra |

## Tip

Seeds pack a great nutritional punch (especially minerals and fiber) and are somewhat lower in fats and carbs than nuts. They are also quite filling, so they make a good snack.

6. Cover and bake in preheated oven for 30 minutes or until the fish is opaque and flakes easily when tested with a fork. Remove fish from the oven and preheat the broiler.

7. Sprinkle the fish mixture with the pumpkin seeds. Broil for 2 minutes or until the seeds are browned.

## Steaming

In many ways, steaming is the ideal cooking method for people with diabetes, as it retains all the nutrients of the food and keeps it deliciously moist without the use of fat. It is also very difficult to overcook food in a steamer, so soggy Brussels sprouts become a thing of the past!

Electric steamers, which give you two baskets so you can steam two different things at the same time, are a good investment — they're just the right size for a single meal and very energy-efficient.

# Cod with Clams and Coconut Milk

## Makes 2 servings

This very simple but festive recipe uses cooked lettuces — not something one normally does, which is a shame, as lettuces retain both flavor and texture very well. Lettuce is also an excellent soporific, so if you are not sleeping well, this could be the dish for you. Serve with steamed new potatoes.

- **Preheat oven to 350°F (180°C)**
- **Ovenproof casserole dish**

| | | |
|---|---|---|
| ½ | small head romaine lettuce, chopped | ½ |
| 1 tbsp | fresh tarragon leaves (or 1 tsp/5 mL dried tarragon) | 15 mL |
| 2 | pieces skinless cod or other white fish fillet (each 3 oz/90 g) | 2 |
| 4 oz | fresh clams, cooked (or frozen or canned) | 125 g |
| Pinch | sea salt | Pinch |
| | Freshly ground black pepper | |
| 6 tbsp | coconut milk | 90 mL |
| 2 tbsp | dry white wine (or 2 tsp/10 mL white wine vinegar) | 30 mL |

1. Spread the chopped lettuce over the bottom of an ovenproof dish large enough to hold the fish. Sprinkle with tarragon.

2. Arrange the fish fillets in rolls or folds over the lettuce. Spoon the clams on top. Sprinkle with salt and pepper.

3. In a bowl, mix the coconut milk and the wine. Pour over the fish.

4. Cover and bake in preheated oven for 30 minutes or until the fish is opaque and flakes easily when tested with a fork.

## NUTRIENTS PER SERVING

| | |
|---|---|
| Calories | 243 |
| Carbohydrate | 7 g |
| Fiber | 2 g |
| Protein | 27 g |
| Fat | 11 g |
| Saturated fat | 9 g |
| Cholesterol | 60 mg |
| Sodium | 176 mg |

### Food Choices

3½  Meat & Alternatives

# Lettuce

Scientists have for some time been working on a way to inject insulin into lettuce, as a direct means of delivering insulin to people with diabetes. Sadly, insulin-bearing lettuce is not yet a reality. Nonetheless, lettuce is a great food choice — it's very low on the glycemic index but very high in vitamins, minerals and fiber.

# Fillet of Cod with Chiles

**Makes 1 serving**

This is a very simple dish but looks and tastes really good. The fieriness of the chile pepper goes well with the cool flavor of the fish; you can add more if you like heat, but be careful not to overdo it. Serve with a wedge of lemon and a green vegetable such as green beans or spinach.

| | | |
|---|---|---|
| 1 tbsp | olive oil | 15 mL |
| 1 | small leek (white and light green parts only), thinly sliced | 1 |
| ½ | bulb fennel, thinly sliced | ½ |
| ½ | small red chile pepper, seeded and cut into very thin slivers | ½ |
| ¾ tsp | dried dillweed (or 2 tsp/10 mL chopped fresh dill) | 3 mL |
| 5 | cherry tomatoes, quartered | 5 |
| 4 oz | skinless cod fillet | 125 g |
| | Freshly ground black pepper | |
| 2 tbsp | white wine (or 1½ tsp/7 mL white wine vinegar) | 30 mL |

1. In a small pan, heat the oil over medium heat. Cook the leek, fennel, chile pepper and dill, stirring often, for 7 to 8 minutes or until the fennel is starting to soften.

2. Add the tomatoes, cover, reduce heat to low and cook gently for 15 minutes.

3. Lay the cod fillet on top of the vegetables and sprinkle with black pepper. Pour the wine around the fish. Cover and cook gently for 5 to 7 minutes or until the fish is opaque and flakes easily when tested with a fork.

## NUTRIENTS PER SERVING

| | |
|---|---|
| Calories | 288 |
| Carbohydrate | 14 g |
| Fiber | 4 g |
| Protein | 22 g |
| Fat | 14 g |
| Saturated fat | 2 g |
| Cholesterol | 52 mg |
| Sodium | 234 mg |

**Food Choices**

| | |
|---|---|
| 3 | Meat & Alternatives |
| 1 | Fat |
| 1 | Extra |

## Sustainable Cod

Because cod is one of the most over-fished and threatened of fish species be careful what you buy. Only buy fish that have good sustainable credentials, the most reliable being that of the Marine Stewardship Council. Look for an oval blue badge with Marine Stewardship Council on it.

# Salmon Steamed with Fennel and Tomatoes

If you have an electric steamer, this is the perfect dish to use it for. If not, you can use a regular steamer basket or even a metal colander over a saucepan. Fish stock or wine will add flavor, but even steaming the dish over a pan of water will be fine. It's an all-in-one dish, so you shouldn't need any extra vegetables.

- **Electric steamer or steamer basket**

| | | |
|---|---|---|
| ¾ cup | dry white wine, unsalted fish stock or water | 175 mL |
| 1 | new potato, thinly sliced | 1 |
| | Freshly ground black pepper | |
| ½ | bulb fennel, trimmed and thinly sliced | ½ |
| 1 | tomato, peeled and thinly sliced | 1 |
| 2 cups | trimmed fresh spinach leaves | 500 mL |
| 3 oz | skinless salmon fillet | 90 g |
| 2 | lemon slices | 2 |

1. Pour the liquid into the lower section of your steamer (or into a saucepan) and bring to a simmer.

2. Arrange the potato slices in the bottom of the steamer basket, overlapping them so that the juices from the other ingredients will not seep through. Season with pepper. Cover and steam for 5 to 8 minutes or until the potatoes are starting to soften.

3. Lay the fennel slices over the potatoes and cover them with the sliced tomato. Cover the tomato with the spinach leaves. Lay the salmon fillet on top of the spinach and the lemon slices on top of the salmon. Cover and steam for 8 to 9 minutes or until the salmon is just opaque and flakes easily when tested with a fork.

4. Warm a plate and carefully lift the salmon, with its bed of vegetables, out onto the plate. Season with a little more pepper and serve immediately.

## NUTRIENTS PER SERVING

| | |
|---|---|
| Calories | 375 |
| Carbohydrate | 31 g |
| Fiber | 5 g |
| Protein | 22 g |
| Fat | 4 g |
| Saturated fat | 1 g |
| Cholesterol | 39 mg |
| Sodium | 217 mg |

### Food Choices

| | |
|---|---|
| 2½ | Meat & Alternatives |
| 1 | Extra |

# Salmon with Asian Greens

This simple dish comes with the vegetables already incorporated. Salmon offers lots of omega-3 fatty acids (good for heart health), nutrients and fiber. Serve with steamed new potatoes.

## Tip

In place of the wine you can substitute 1 tbsp (15 mL) white wine vinegar and ¼ cup (60 mL) no-salt-added ready-to-use vegetable or chicken broth.

| | | |
|---|---|---|
| 1 tbsp | olive or sunflower oil | 15 mL |
| 1 | stalk celery, chopped | 1 |
| 2 cups | roughly chopped choi sum, bok choy or other leafy Asian greens | 500 mL |
| ½ | small bulb fennel | ½ |
| 3 cups | trimmed fresh spinach leaves | 750 mL |
| 3 | slices lemon | 3 |
| 3 oz | skinless salmon fillet | 90 g |
| | Freshly ground black pepper | |
| ¼ cup | dry white wine (see tip, at left) | 60 mL |

1. In a large saucepan, heat the oil over medium heat. Cook the celery, choi sum and fennel, stirring often, for 5 to 10 minutes or until they have started to soften.

2. Add the spinach and cook until it wilts.

3. Lay 2 of the lemon slices over the spinach mixture. Lay the fish over the lemon. Season lightly with pepper. Pour the wine around the fish. Reduce heat to low, cover tightly and simmer gently for 10 to 15 minutes or until the salmon is just opaque and flakes easily when tested with a fork. Remove the fish from the pan and set aside.

4. Arrange the vegetables on a serving plate and drizzle with the cooking juices. Lay the salmon on top and decorate with the remaining lemon slice.

## NUTRIENTS PER SERVING

| | |
|---|---|
| Calories | 346 |
| Carbohydrate | 15 g |
| Fiber | 6 g |
| Protein | 24 g |
| Fat | 18 g |
| Saturated fat | 3 g |
| Cholesterol | 39 mg |
| Sodium | 359 mg |

### Food Choices

| | |
|---|---|
| 2½ | Meat & Alternatives |
| 2 | Fat |
| 1 | Extra |

# Fettuccine with Smoked Salmon and Cream Sauce

## Tips

Because this recipe is high in fat, it should be a special occasion treat on days when your fat consumption at other meals is low.

Soy or oat cream, both of which are low in saturated fat and cholesterol-free, will taste just as good in this dish as cream made from cow's milk, so try them if you're concerned about your fat or cholesterol intake.

### NUTRIENTS PER SERVING

| | |
|---|---|
| Calories | 603 |
| Carbohydrate | 63 g |
| Fiber | 3 g |
| Protein | 23 g |
| Fat | 24 g |
| Saturated fat | 9 g |
| Cholesterol | 53 mg |
| Sodium | 478 mg |

### Food Choices

| | |
|---|---|
| 3½ | Carbohydrate |
| 1½ | Meat & Alternatives |
| 3 | Fat |
| ½ | Extra |

| | | |
|---|---|---|
| 2 tsp | olive oil | 10 mL |
| 2 | mushrooms, thinly sliced | 2 |
| ¼ cup | dry white wine (or 1 tbsp/15 mL white wine vinegar) | 60 mL |
| ¼ cup | light (5%) cream (or non-dairy cream) | 60 mL |
| 2 oz | smoked salmon, cut into thin strips | 60 g |
| | Juice of ½ lemon | |
| | Freshly ground black pepper | |
| 3 oz | fresh fettuccine or other long pasta (or 2½ oz/75 g dried) | 90 g |
| ½ tsp | chopped fresh dill (see tip, at left) | 2 mL |

1. In a small pan, heat the oil over medium heat. Cook the mushrooms, stirring often, for 2 to 3 minutes or until they start to release their juice. Do not let them color.

2. Add the wine, increase the heat to medium-high and cook for 2 minutes to reduce the wine.

3. Remove from heat and add the cream and salmon. Season to taste with salt and pepper, and drizzle with lemon juice. Cover and keep warm.

4. In a pot of boiling water, cook the pasta according to the package instructions, omitting salt, until it is just al dente.

5. Gently mix the sauce into the pasta and sprinkle with dill.

# Baked Trout with Apple

This dish works really well with a baked potato to soak up the delicious juices and a green vegetable.

## Tip

In place of the wine, you can substitute 1 tbsp (15 mL) white wine vinegar and 3 tbsp (45 mL) unsalted fish stock or no-salt-added ready-to-use vegetable or chicken broth.

| | | |
|---|---|---|
| 1 tsp | olive oil | 5 mL |
| 1 | small onion, thinly sliced | 1 |
| 1 | small tart cooking apple, peeled and sliced | 1 |
| 1 | sprig fresh rosemary, leaves chopped (or 1/2 tsp/2 mL dried rosemary) | 1 |
| Pinch | sea salt or seaweed condiment | Pinch |
| | Freshly ground black pepper | |
| 3 oz | trout, salmon or arctic char fillet (skinless, if desired) | 90 g |
| 1/4 cup | dry white wine (see tip, at left) | 60 mL |

1. In a large frying pan, heat the oil over medium-low heat. Add the onion and apple, cover the pan and cook gently for 15 minutes or until they are quite soft. Add the rosemary and season with a pinch of salt and with pepper to taste.

2. Lay the fish on top of the onion mixture and pour the wine around it. Cover and cook gently for 10 to 15 minutes or until the fish flakes easily when tested with a fork.

**NUTRIENTS PER SERVING**

| | |
|---|---|
| Calories | 274 |
| Carbohydrate | 26 g |
| Fiber | 3 g |
| Protein | 16 g |
| Fat | 8 g |
| Saturated fat | 2 g |
| Cholesterol | 71 mg |
| Sodium | 211 mg |

**Food Choices**

| | |
|---|---|
| 1 | Carbohydrate |
| 2 | Meat & Alternatives |
| 1/2 | Extra |

# Poached Trout with Rhubarb Sauce

Serve with mashed potato or sweet potato and a green vegetable.

## Tip

If you are concerned about your fat intake, try using soy or oat cream in place of cow's milk cream. Both are low in fat, and they taste remarkably good, especially in a dish like this. They are available at well-stocked supermarkets and most health food stores.

| NUTRIENTS PER SERVING | |
|---|---|
| Calories | 248 |
| Carbohydrate | 5 g |
| Fiber | 0 g |
| Protein | 17 g |
| Fat | 14 g |
| Saturated fat | 8 g |
| Cholesterol | 82 mg |
| Sodium | 168 mg |
| **Food Choices** | |
| 2 Meat & Alternatives | |
| 1½ Fat | |

**• Food processor**

| 1 | rainbow trout fillet | 1 |
|---|---|---|
| 2 | slices lemon | 2 |
| 6 tbsp | dry white wine or water | 90 mL |
| 1 tbsp | butter | 15 mL |
| ½ cup | chopped fresh rhubarb | 125 mL |
| ¼ cup | light (5%) cream (or oat or soy cream) | 60 mL |
| | Juice of ½ lemon | |
| Pinch | sea salt | Pinch |
| | Freshly ground white pepper | |

1. Heat a saucepan big enough to hold the trout over medium-low heat. Add the fish, lemon slices and wine, cover and cook for 8 to 10 minutes or until the fish flakes easily when tested with a fork.

2. Meanwhile, in a small saucepan, melt the butter over medium-low heat. Stir in the rhubarb, cover and cook until tender.

3. Transfer the rhubarb to the food processor and add the cream, lemon juice, salt and pepper to taste. Purée until smooth. The sauce should be the consistency of double cream; if it is too thick, add some of the cooking juices from the fish.

4. To serve, skin the fish and lay on a plate. Spoon the sauce over top.

# Tuna with Beets and Red Cabbage

## Makes 2 servings

This vigorous dish, with strong flavors and colors, is ideal to set you up for a long winter walk! The contrast of the warm vegetables and the cold tuna works well. Serve with crusty whole-grain bread.

## Tip

Look for a vegetable broth with less than 20 g of sodium per ⅔ cup (150 mL), or make your own with no added salt.

## NUTRIENTS PER SERVING

| | |
|---|---|
| Calories | 270 |
| Carbohydrate | 29 g |
| Fiber | 4 g |
| Protein | 26 g |
| Fat | 6 g |
| Saturated fat | 2 g |
| Cholesterol | 47 mg |
| Sodium | 210 mg |

### Food Choices

| | |
|---|---|
| 1½ | Carbohydrate |
| 3 | Meat & Alternatives |
| 1 | Fat |

- **Steamer basket**
- **Pie dish**

| | | |
|---|---|---|
| 1 | beet, peeled and quartered | 1 |
| 1 | small oblong baking potato, cut into eighths | 1 |
| Pinch | sea salt | Pinch |
| | Freshly ground black pepper | |
| 1 cup | thinly sliced red cabbage | 250 mL |
| ½ | small tart cooking apple, finely diced | ½ |
| ½ tsp | coriander seeds, lightly crushed | 2 mL |
| ¼ cup | no-salt-added ready-to-use vegetable broth or water | 60 mL |
| ⅔ cup | low-fat plain yogurt (cow's, goat's, sheep's or soy) | 150 mL |
| 1 | can (6 oz/170 g) low-sodium water-packed light tuna, drained and flaked | 1 |

1. In a steamer basket set over a saucepan of simmering water, steam the beet and potato for 10 to 15 minutes or until tender. Mash them together, then season with a pinch of salt and with pepper to taste. Spread the mashed vegetables in a layer in the bottom of a pie dish and keep warm.

2. Meanwhile, in a small saucepan, combine the cabbage, apple, coriander seeds and broth. Cover and cook gently over medium-low heat for 5 to 8 minutes or until the apple is cooked through and the cabbage is cooked but still slightly crunchy.

3. Remove the cabbage mixture from the heat and stir in two-thirds of the yogurt. Spread over the mashed vegetables.

4. Arrange the tuna on top and drizzle with the rest of the yogurt. Season with pepper to taste.

# Beets

Because of their relatively high sugar content, people with diabetes tend to veer away from beets, but provided you eat the whole root (and not just the juice) and combine them with other low-GI foods, beets' benefits far outweigh their sugar content. They are very high in vitamins A, $B_1$, $B_2$, $B_6$ and C, choline, folate, iodine, manganese, potassium and fiber, and are well known as excellent cleansers of the blood. And they taste great!

# Stir-Fried Tuna with Snow Peas

Stir-fries are great if you are cooking for one or two, as they are very energy-efficient and quick to prepare — not to mention tasty, nutritious and low-fat. This is quite a substantial meal, but if you feel you need it, accompany it with quinoa or brown rice (do not forget that the rice will take a lot longer to cook than the stir-fry).

| | | |
|---|---|---|
| 1 tbsp | vegetable oil | 15 mL |
| 2 | drained canned anchovy fillets | 2 |
| 2 | cloves garlic, halved if they are very large | 2 |
| ½ | small red chile pepper, seeded and thinly sliced | ½ |
| 1 | 1-inch (2.5 cm) piece gingerroot, peeled and cut into thin matchsticks | 1 |
| 1 cup | packed choi sum, bok choy or other Chinese greens, roughly chopped | 250 mL |
| ½ cup | snow peas, trimmed and halved | 125 mL |
| 3 oz | skinless tuna steak, cut into large dice | 90 g |
| | Juice of ½ lime | |
| 3 | green onions, trimmed and roughly chopped | 3 |

1. In a wok or wide frying pan, heat the oil over medium-high heat. Add the anchovies, garlic, chile and ginger and stir-fry for 3 to 5 minutes.

2. Add the greens, reduce the heat to medium, cover and cook for 3 minutes or until the greens are well wilted but not overcooked.

3. Add the snow peas, cover and cook for 2 minutes or until slightly softened but still crunchy.

4. Add the tuna, increase the heat to medium-high and stir-fry for 1 to 3 minutes or until tuna is browned on all sides and cooked to desired doneness.

5. Drizzle with the lime juice and sprinkle with green onions. Serve immediately.

## NUTRIENTS PER SERVING

| | |
|---|---|
| Calories | 311 |
| Carbohydrate | 18 g |
| Fiber | 4 g |
| Protein | 27 g |
| Fat | 16 g |
| Saturated fat | 2 g |
| Cholesterol | 45 mg |
| Sodium | 387 mg |

### Food Choices

| | |
|---|---|
| 3 | Meat & Alternatives |
| 1 | Fat |
| 1 | Extra |

# Moules Marinières

**Makes 1 serving**

Serve with crusty brown bread and a green salad.

## Tips

In place of the wine, you can substitute 1 tbsp (15 mL) white wine vinegar and $1/3$ cup (75 mL) unsalted fish stock or no-salt-added ready-to-use vegetable or chicken broth.

Because this recipe is high in fat and sodium, it should be a special occasion treat on days when your fat and sodium consumption at other meals is low.

| | | |
|---|---|---|
| 12 oz | fresh mussels in their shells | 375 g |
| 1 tbsp | unsalted butter | 15 mL |
| $1/2$ | small onion, finely chopped | $1/2$ |
| $1/2$ | clove garlic, crushed | $1/2$ |
| $1/2$ cup | dry white wine (see tip, at left) | 125 mL |
| | Freshly ground black pepper | |
| 1 tsp | chopped fresh parsley | 5 mL |

1. Clean the mussels thoroughly, scraping off as many of the barnacles as possible and removing the beard (or byssus) from the pointed end. They should all close firmly when tapped; discard any that don't, as it means they are dead and will make you ill if eaten.

2. Heat a pan large enough to hold the mussels over medium heat. Add the butter, onion, garlic, wine and several grinds of black pepper. Bring to a simmer, then add the mussels. Reduce heat to medium-low, cover, give the pan a good shake and simmer for 5 minutes or until mussels have opened.

3. Warm a large bowl. Remove the pan from the heat and, using a ladle, spoon the mussels and cooking juices into the bowl. (If you pour the juices, the sand that inevitably remains in mussels goes into the bowl too). Discard any mussels that have not opened.

4. Sprinkle with the chopped parsley and serve immediately.

| NUTRIENTS PER SERVING | |
|---|---|
| Calories | 360 |
| Carbohydrate | 15 g |
| Fiber | 1 g |
| Protein | 13 g |
| Fat | 19 g |
| Saturated fat | 9 g |
| Cholesterol | 57 mg |
| Sodium | 584 mg |
| **Food Choices** | |
| $1 1/2$ Meat & Alternatives | |
| $2 1/2$ Fat | |

# Stir-Fried Shrimp with Ginger

This quick, easy and delicious way to cook shrimp works well for just one person. Serve on a bed of lettuce, with a slice of crusty whole-grain bread or cooked brown rice.

## Tip

Lime juice, with its slightly sweeter flavor, makes a nice change from lemon juice.

| | | |
|---|---|---|
| 3 | green onions | 3 |
| 1 tbsp | vegetable oil | 15 mL |
| 1 tbsp | slivered gingerroot | 15 mL |
| ½ cup | sliced mushrooms | 125 mL |
| 4 oz | large shrimp, peeled and deveined | 125 g |
| | Juice of 1 lime | |
| Pinch | sea salt | Pinch |
| | Freshly ground black pepper | |

1. Slice the green part of the green onions lengthwise into very thin matchsticks. Slice the white part into thin matchsticks and keep them separate.

2. In a wok or wide frying pan, heat the oil over medium-high heat. Stir-fry the ginger for 2 minutes.

3. Add the mushrooms and stir-fry for 1 minute.

4. Add the shrimp and the white part of the green onions and stir-fry for 2 to 3 minutes or until shrimp are pink, firm and opaque.

5. Stir in the green part of the green onion and the lime juice. Season with a pinch of salt and with pepper to taste. Serve immediately.

## NUTRIENTS PER SERVING

| | |
|---|---|
| Calories | 254 |
| Carbohydrate | 9 g |
| Fiber | 3 g |
| Protein | 25 g |
| Fat | 14 g |
| Saturated fat | 2 g |
| Cholesterol | 182 mg |
| Sodium | 301 mg |

### Food Choices

| | |
|---|---|
| 3 | Meat & Alternatives |
| 1 | Fat |
| ½ | Extra |

# New Orleans Jambalaya

A jambalaya is a somewhat spicy stew traditionally served with rice.

## Tip

Look for a chicken broth with less than 40 g of sodium per ⅔ cup (150 mL), or make your own with no added salt.

| | | |
|---|---|---|
| 1 tbsp | vegetable oil | 15 mL |
| 4 oz | boneless skinless chicken thighs (about 2), cut into chunks | 125 g |
| ¼ cup | diced smoked ham | 60 mL |
| 1 | onion, finely chopped | 1 |
| 1 | stalk celery, finely chopped | 1 |
| 1 | red bell pepper, finely chopped | 1 |
| 1 | dried chile pepper, crumbled | 1 |
| 1½ tsp | dried thyme | 7 mL |
| 2 | bay leaves | 2 |
| 1 | can (14 oz/398 mL) no-salt-added diced tomatoes | 1 |
| ¼ cup | no-salt-added or reduced-sodium ready-to-use chicken broth | 60 mL |
| 4 | large shrimp, peeled and deveined | 4 |
| Pinch | sea salt | Pinch |
| | Freshly ground black pepper | |
| 4 | green onions, chopped | 4 |

1. In a large saucepan, heat the oil over medium heat. Cook the chicken and ham, stirring often, for 2 minutes.

2. Add the onion, celery and red pepper, and cook, stirring often, for 5 minutes.

3. Stir in the chile pepper, thyme, bay leaves and tomatoes, and cook for 3 minutes.

4. Add the chicken broth and bring to a boil. Reduce the heat and simmer for 10 to 15 minutes to allow the flavors to blend.

5. Add the shrimp and simmer for about 5 minutes or until shrimp are pink, firm and opaque. Discard bay leaves. Season with a pinch of salt and with pepper to taste. Sprinkle with green onions.

## NUTRIENTS PER SERVING

| | |
|---|---|
| Calories | 180 |
| Carbohydrate | 18 g |
| Fiber | 4 g |
| Protein | 31 g |
| Fat | 16 g |
| Saturated fat | 2 g |
| Cholesterol | 163 mg |
| Sodium | 274 mg |

### Food Choices

| | |
|---|---|
| ½ | Carbohydrate |
| 4 | Meat & Alternatives |
| ½ | Extra |

# Chicken and Eggs

Oven-Baked Chicken with Split Peas. . . . . . . . . . . 74

Chicken with Anchovies and Cauliflower. . . . . . . . 76

Pan-Fried Chicken with Okra. . . . . . . . . . . . . . 78

Chicken with Artichoke Hearts . . . . . . . . . . . . . 80

Pomegranate Chicken . . . . . . . . . . . . . . . . . . 82

Chicken with Avocado and Earl Grey Tea . . . . . . . 84

Chicken with Ginger and Water Chestnuts . . . . . . 85

Herb Frittata . . . . . . . . . . . . . . . . . . . . . . . 86

Butternut Squash and Baked Eggs . . . . . . . . . . . 88

Lentil and Egg Pie . . . . . . . . . . . . . . . . . . . . 89

# Oven-Baked Chicken with Split Peas

**Makes 2 servings**

This is a great one-pot meal, good at any time of year but especially in winter. And it provides you with a built-in second meal of chicken soup (see box, opposite). Serve with a green vegetable or a salad.

## Tip

Look for a chicken broth with less than 40 g of sodium per ⅔ cup (150 mL), or make your own with no added salt.

### NUTRIENTS PER SERVING

| | |
|---|---|
| Calories | 632 |
| Carbohydrate | 67 g |
| Fiber | 29 g |
| Protein | 58 g |
| Fat | 15 g |
| Saturated fat | 2 g |
| Cholesterol | 115 mg |
| Sodium | 238 mg |

### Food Choices

| | |
|---|---|
| 2 | Carbohydrate |
| 8 | Meat & Alternatives |
| 1 | Fat |
| 2 | Extra |

**• Large ovenproof saucepan**

| | | |
|---|---|---|
| 1 cup | yellow split peas, rinsed | 250 mL |
| | Cold water | |
| 1 tbsp | olive oil | 15 mL |
| 1 | leek (white and light green parts only), trimmed and sliced | 1 |
| 2 | cloves garlic, sliced | 2 |
| 1 | 1- to 2-inch (2.5 to 5 cm) piece gingerroot, peeled and cut into matchsticks | 1 |
| ¾ cup | no-salt-added or reduced-sodium ready-to-use chicken broth | 175 mL |
| 1 tsp | whole black peppercorns | 5 mL |
| ½ tsp | dried herbes de Provence | 2 mL |
| Pinch | sea salt | Pinch |
| ½ | small chicken (cut lengthwise through the back and left in one piece) | ½ |

1. Place the split peas in a large bowl with enough cold water to cover. Soak for 3 to 4 hours.

2. Strain off the water, transfer the peas to a pot and cover with fresh cold water. Bring to a boil, then reduce the heat and simmer for 30 minutes. Strain off the water and set the peas aside.

3. In an ovenproof saucepan big enough to hold the chicken lying flat, heat the oil over medium-low heat. Cook the leek, garlic and ginger, stirring often, for 10 minutes or until quite soft.

4. Add the soaked split peas, broth, peppercorns, herbes de Provence and salt. Place the chicken in the pan, cut side down, so that it sinks into the peas and broth. Reduce heat to low, cover and simmer for 40 minutes.

## Tips

If fresh gingerroot is not available, substitute 1 to 2 tsp (5 to 10 mL) ground ginger. Add the ground ginger with the herbes de Provence instead of with the leek.

If you are not able to buy a half chicken, buy a whole one. With a pair of scissors and a knife, you should be able to cut it in half, even if it is a bit untidy. Use half for this dish and freeze the other half for future use.

5. Meanwhile, preheat the oven to 350°F (180°C).

6. Remove the lid from the pan and transfer the pot to the oven. Bake for 40 minutes or until the top of the chicken is browned and crisp.

7. Remove the chicken from the pot to a cutting board and carve the chicken. Use a slotted spoon to serve the peas with the chicken.

## Second-Day Chicken Soup

When the meal is over, strip any remaining chicken from the carcass, discarding the bones and skin, and return the meat to the pot. Add $1\frac{1}{4}$ cups (300 mL) no-salt-added or reduced-sodium ready-to-use chicken broth and a bouquet garni (see tip, page 81). Bring to a boil, then reduce the heat and simmer for 45 to 60 minutes. Discard the bouquet garni. Let the soup cool, then ladle it into an airtight container and refrigerate it overnight. Reheat over medium heat until steaming.

# Chicken with Anchovies and Cauliflower

This is the simplest but tastiest of chicken dishes. Cauliflower somehow goes particularly well with anchovies, but you can use broccoli if you prefer. Serve with a green vegetable.

## Tip

The remaining anchovies can be stored in their oil in the fridge for up to 3 days. Use as a seasoning with beef, in an omelet or as an alternative to salt in a salad dressing.

| NUTRIENTS PER SERVING | |
| --- | --- |
| Calories | 291 |
| Carbohydrate | 7 g |
| Fiber | 2 g |
| Protein | 28 g |
| Fat | 18 g |
| Saturated fat | 3 g |
| Cholesterol | 79 mg |
| Sodium | 442 mg |
| **Food Choices** | |
| 3½ | Meat & Alternatives |
| 3 | Fat |
| 1 | Extra |

### Steamer basket

| | | |
| --- | --- | --- |
| 1 tbsp | oil from anchovies and/or olive oil | 15 mL |
| 1 | small skinless chicken breast (or 2 thighs or drumsticks), patted dry | 1 |
| 2 to 3 | drained canned anchovy fillets, finely chopped | 2 to 3 |
| ½ | small cauliflower, broken into florets | ½ |
| ½ | lemon, cut in half | ½ |
| | Freshly ground black pepper | |

1. In a small frying pan, heat the oil over medium heat. Cook the anchovies for 2 minutes, breaking them up.

2. Add the chicken and increase the heat to medium-high. Cook, turning, until the chicken is nicely browned on all sides. Reduce the heat to medium-low, cover tightly and cook for 15 minutes or until the chicken is no longer pink inside.

3. Meanwhile, in a steamer basket placed over a saucepan of simmering water, steam the cauliflower for about 5 minutes or until tender-crisp.

4. Remove the lid from the chicken and squeeze over the juice from one-quarter lemon. (Save the remaining quarter in case you would like an extra squeeze of lemon juice when you taste the dish.)

5. Arrange the chicken and steamed cauliflower on a warmed plate. Pour the juices from the pan over. Season with black pepper and serve immediately.

# Cauliflower

Cauliflower is one of those vegetables, like beets, that you either love or hate. Even though it has an almost starchy texture, it is very low in carbohydrate. Moreover, it contains useful amounts of protein, thiamin, riboflavin, niacin, magnesium, phosphorus, dietary fiber, vitamin C, vitamin K, vitamin $B_6$, folate, pantothenic acid, potassium and manganese.

# Pan-Fried Chicken with Okra

This is an easy, quick and colorful dish that works well for one; double up the ingredients if there are two of you. Serve on its own, or with rice and a salad if you are really hungry.

| | | |
|---|---|---|
| 1 tbsp | sunflower oil | 15 mL |
| 1 | small skinless chicken breast (or 2 thighs or drumsticks) | 1 |
| 2 | pieces okra, trimmed and roughly chopped | 2 |
| 2 | drained canned baby sweet corn cobs, halved (or 1/4 cup/60 mL drained corn kernels, thawed if frozen) | 2 |
| 1 | zucchini, thickly sliced | 1 |
| 1/2 cup | canned diced tomatoes, with juice | 125 mL |
| 1/4 cup | red wine or no-salt-added or reduced-sodium ready-to-use vegetable broth | 60 mL |
| 1/2 tsp | dried marjoram | 2 mL |
| | Freshly ground black pepper | |
| | Freshly squeezed lemon juice | |

1. In a saucepan, heat the oil over medium-high heat. Cook the chicken, turning, until nicely browned on all sides.

2. Add the okra, corn and zucchini and cook until the vegetables have also taken on a little color.

3. Add the tomatoes, wine and marjoram, and season with pepper. Bring to a boil, then reduce heat to medium-low, cover and simmer for 20 minutes or until the chicken is no longer pink inside.

4. Drizzle with lemon juice to taste before serving.

## NUTRIENTS PER SERVING

| | |
|---|---|
| Calories | 381 |
| Carbohydrate | 20 g |
| Fiber | 4 g |
| Protein | 28 g |
| Fat | 18 g |
| Saturated fat | 2 g |
| Cholesterol | 73 mg |
| Sodium | 450 mg |

### Food Choices

| | |
|---|---|
| 1 | Carbohydrate |
| 3 1/2 | Meat & Alternatives |
| 2 1/2 | Fat |

# Okra

Okra is a great vegetable for people with diabetes, as the slightly gluey juices are very good for helping to regulate blood sugar. Even better, it is very nutritious, containing significant amounts of folate, calcium, fiber, iron, vitamin A, vitamin C, potassium and magnesium.

# Chicken with Artichoke Hearts

**Makes 2 servings**

You can buy quite small pieces of turkey in most supermarkets now — just enough for two — if you want a change from chicken. This sauce goes equally well with both birds. Serve with new potatoes or mashed white and sweet potatoes and a green vegetable, such as broccoli or spinach.

| | | |
|---|---|---|
| 8 oz | boneless skinless chicken breasts or turkey breast | 250 g |
| 1 | small onion | 1 |
| ½ | carrot | ½ |
| 2 | mushrooms | 2 |
| | Bouquet garni (see tip, at left) | |
| | Whole black peppercorns | |
| 2 cups | water | 500 mL |
| 1 tbsp | olive oil | 15 mL |
| 1 | medium onion, thinly sliced | 1 |
| 1 | small stalk celery, finely chopped | 1 |
| 1 tbsp | all-purpose flour | 15 mL |
| 4 | artichoke hearts (freshly cooked, frozen or canned), well drained and halved or quartered | 4 |
| | Grated zest and juice of 1 small orange | |
| 1 | small orange, peeled and cut into segments | 1 |
| | Freshly ground black pepper | |

1. Place chicken, small onion, carrot, mushrooms, bouquet garni and water in a large saucepan. Bring to a boil over medium heat. Reduce heat and simmer for 20 minutes or chicken is no longer pink inside.

2 Transfer the meat to a plate and set aside. Strain the stock, discarding the bouquet garni and other solids, and set the stock aside.

3. In another saucepan, heat the oil over medium heat. Cook the sliced onion and celery, stirring often, until softened. Add the flour and cook, stirring, for 1 minute.

## NUTRIENTS PER SERVING

| | |
|---|---|
| Calories | 288 |
| Carbohydrate | 22 g |
| Fiber | 3 g |
| Protein | 28 g |
| Fat | 10 g |
| Saturated fat | 2 g |
| Cholesterol | 73 mg |
| Sodium | 295 mg |

### Food Choices

| | |
|---|---|
| ½ | Carbohydrate |
| 3½ | Meat & Alternatives |
| ½ | Fat |

## Tip

To make a bouquet garni, tie together fresh parsley and thyme sprigs and a bay leaf (or place them in a cheesecloth bag). If fresh herbs are not available, use a mixture of dried herbs tied in cheesecloth or placed in a tea infuser.

4. Gradually stir in $1/2$ cup (125 mL) of the reserved stock. Stir in artichoke hearts, orange zest and orange juice. Cook for 2 minutes. Add the reserved chicken and cook until heated through.

5. Serve decorated with the orange segments.

## Artichoke Hearts

Artichoke hearts are a great way to add interest to a dish, as they have a distinct flavor and are very versatile: they can be used in a hot dish, a salad or a dip. They have a small amount of fat but high levels of fiber, vitamins $B_6$, C and K, folate, magnesium, potassium, copper, manganese, niacin, iron and phosphorus.

Fresh globe artichokes are delicious but quite seasonal. Fortunately, canned and frozen artichoke hearts are available all year round and are easier to use if you are incorporating them into a dish rather than eating them on their own.

# Pomegranate Chicken

**Makes 1 serving**

Since this dish is made with leftover cooked chicken, it's ready to eat in a flash! Serve with crusty whole-grain bread or steamed new potatoes.

| ¼ cup | plain yogurt (cow's, sheep's, goat's or soy) | 60 mL |
| 1 tbsp | fresh pomegranate seeds | 15 mL |
| | Freshly squeezed lemon juice | |
| Pinch | sea salt | Pinch |
| | Freshly ground black pepper | |
| | Boiling water | |
| | Lettuce leaves | |
| 1 | cooked skinless chicken breast or leg quarter, sliced and warmed | 1 |

1. In a bowl, combine yogurt and pomegranate seeds, stirring well. Stir in lemon juice to taste, then season with a pinch of salt and with pepper to taste. Thin the sauce slightly with a little boiling water.

2. Arrange the lettuce on a plate, arrange the chicken slices on top of the leaves and spoon the sauce over top.

## Simple Marinade for Lamb, Chicken or Fish

In a bowl, whisk together lemon juice, good-quality olive oil, a little sea salt and some freshly ground black pepper. Add lamb, chicken or fish and marinate for 30 minutes before cooking. This simple marinade gives the meat or fish a more interesting flavor and prevents it from drying out while cooking. For a different flavor, add a little bit of reduced-sodium soy sauce to the marinade.

### NUTRIENTS PER SERVING

| | |
|---|---|
| Calories | 180 |
| Carbohydrate | 7 g |
| Fiber | 1 g |
| Protein | 28 g |
| Fat | 4 g |
| Saturated fat | 1 g |
| Cholesterol | 76 mg |
| Sodium | 247 mg |

**Food Choices**

½ Carbohydrate
3½ Meat & Alternatives

# Pomegranate Seeds

While pomegranate juice, like all fruit juices, is bad news for people with diabetes because the sugars have been "liberated" and are easily accessible, the fruit itself is fine in moderation. Indeed, pomegranate seeds offer a high level of antioxidants! You should also be able to buy fresh pomegranate seeds, but if not, buy a whole pomegranate and use the remaining seeds on cereal or as a dessert with yogurt. Dried pomegranate seeds are another option. Look for them in Middle Eastern grocery stores and soak them for 15 minutes in boiling water before use.

# Chicken with Avocado and Earl Grey Tea

Earl Grey tea gives a pleasantly smoky flavor to this refreshing sauce.

## Tip

Avocados are high in monounsaturated fats, good not only for heart health but also for improving insulin sensitivity — and they taste wonderful!

| | | |
|---|---|---|
| 1 | Earl Grey tea bag | 1 |
| 1/3 cup | boiling water | 75 mL |
| 1 | large boneless skinless chicken breast (or 2 small), thinly sliced | 1 |
| 1 | small leek (white and light green parts only), trimmed and very thinly sliced | 1 |
| 1 tsp | drained green peppercorns (optional) | 5 mL |
| 2 tbsp | low-fat plain yogurt (cow's, sheep's, goat's or soy) | 30 mL |
| | Freshly squeezed lemon juice | |
| Pinch | sea salt | Pinch |
| | Freshly ground black pepper | |
| 1 | avocado | 1 |
| | Mixed leafy greens (lettuce, lamb's lettuce, watercress, arugula, parsley, etc.) | |

1. Place the teabag in a bowl and pour in boiling water. Let steep for 3 to 5 minutes, to desired strength, then discard the bag.

2. In a medium saucepan, combine tea, chicken, leek and peppercorns (if using). Bring to a boil, then reduce heat to low, cover and simmer for 5 to 8 minutes or until the chicken is no longer pink inside. Using a slotted spoon, transfer the chicken and leek to a bowl, reserving the cooking juices.

3. In a bowl, stir the yogurt until smooth, then add the cooking juices and lemon juice to taste. Season with a pinch of salt and with pepper to taste.

4. Peel and slice the avocado. Add to the chicken mixture, then drizzle with some of the sauce.

5. To serve, pile the leafy greens on a plate. Pile the chicken and avocado mixture in the middle. Pour the remaining sauce over top.

## NUTRIENTS PER SERVING

| | |
|---|---|
| Calories | 327 |
| Carbohydrate | 16 g |
| Fiber | 8 g |
| Protein | 28 g |
| Fat | 18 g |
| Saturated fat | 3 g |
| Cholesterol | 74 mg |
| Sodium | 232 mg |

### Food Choices

| | |
|---|---|
| 3½ | Meat & Alternatives |
| 1 | Extra |

# Chicken with Ginger and Water Chestnuts

**Makes 1 serving**

If you're making this Asian-inspired recipe for two, simply double the ingredients. The water chestnuts add a lovely fresh crunch. Serve with mashed root vegetables and a green vegetable, such as broccoli, green beans or spinach.

## Tip

Ginger is a great spice to cook with and, in traditional Eastern medicine, it is used to assist in digestion and in blood sugar control.

### NUTRIENTS PER SERVING

| | |
|---|---|
| Calories | 326 |
| Carbohydrate | 22 g |
| Fiber | 3 g |
| Protein | 25 g |
| Fat | 15 g |
| Saturated fat | 4 g |
| Cholesterol | 73 mg |
| Sodium | 227 mg |

### Food Choices

| | |
|---|---|
| ½ | Carbohydrate |
| 3½ | Meat & Alternatives |
| 1 | Fat |

- Preheat oven to 375°F (190°C)
- Small baking pan with a rack

| | | |
|---|---|---|
| 1 | small skin-on bone-in chicken breast (about 6 oz/175 g) | 1 |
| 1 | can (4 oz/125 mL) water-packed water chestnuts | 1 |
| 1 tsp | olive oil | 5 mL |
| 1 tbsp | slivered gingerroot | 15 mL |
| ¼ cup | freshly squeezed orange juice | 60 mL |
| Pinch | sea salt | Pinch |
| | Freshly ground black pepper | |

1. Place the chicken skin side up on the rack in the baking pan. Roast in preheated oven for 25 minutes or until no longer pink inside. Transfer to a warm plate and tent with foil to keep warm.

2. Drain the water chestnuts, reserving 2 tbsp (30 mL) of the water from the can. Cut each water chestnut slice in half.

3. In a small pan, heat the oil over medium heat. Cook the ginger, stirring often, for 2 to 3 minutes or until softened.

4. Add the chicken to the pan, along with the water chestnuts, the reserved water from the can and the orange juice. Reduce the heat and simmer gently for 3 to 4 minutes to amalgamate the flavors. Season with a pinch of salt and with pepper to taste. Serve immediately.

# Herb Frittata

This omelet is perfect for summertime, when fresh herbs are readily available. It can be eaten warm or cool, cut into wedges and served with a salad. Even if you are only catering for one, you'll be happy to have leftovers for the next day's lunch. Serve with crusty bread.

- **Steamer basket**
- **Ovenproof skillet or omelet pan**

| | | |
|---|---|---|
| 1 tbsp | olive oil, divided | 15 mL |
| 1 | small leek (white and light green parts only), trimmed and thinly sliced | 1 |
| 1 | clove garlic, sliced | 1 |
| ½ cup | chopped green beans or green peas (fresh or frozen) | 125 mL |
| 3 | large eggs | 3 |
| 2 tbsp | water | 30 mL |
| 1 cup | trimmed spinach leaves | 250 mL |
| 1 cup | trimmed watercress | 250 mL |
| 2 | leaves fresh mint, chopped | 2 |
| 2 | sprigs fresh parsley, trimmed and chopped | 2 |
| 1 | sprig fresh cilantro, trimmed and chopped (optional) | 1 |
| 1 tbsp | pine nuts | 15 mL |
| Pinch | sea salt | Pinch |
| | Freshly ground black pepper | |
| 1 tbsp | freshly grated Parmesan cheese | 15 mL |

1. In a small frying pan, heat half of the oil over medium-low heat. Cook the leek and garlic, stirring often, until very soft.

2. Meanwhile, in a steamer basket set over a saucepan of simmering water, steam the beans just until tender-crisp. Set aside.

## NUTRIENTS PER SERVING

| | |
|---|---|
| Calories | 252 |
| Carbohydrate | 11 g |
| Fiber | 2 g |
| Protein | 13 g |
| Fat | 18 g |
| Saturated fat | 4 g |
| Cholesterol | 281 mg |
| Sodium | 248 mg |

### Food Choices

| | |
|---|---|
| 1½ | Meat & Alternatives |
| 2½ | Fat |

## Tip

To clean leeks, split them in half lengthwise and submerge them in warm water, moving them around to remove all traces of dirt. Transfer to a colander and rinse thoroughly under cold water.

**3.** In a large bowl, beat together the eggs and water. Add the leek and garlic, beans, spinach, watercress, mint, parsley, cilantro, pine nuts and salt. Season with pepper to taste.

**4.** Preheat the broiler.

**5.** In the ovenproof skillet or omelet pan, heat the remaining oil over medium-high heat until almost smoking. Pour in the egg mixture and cook for 2 minutes or until the bottom of the omelet is set. Sprinkle the top with Parmesan.

**6.** Place the pan under the broiler until the top of the omelet is set and browned (take care that it does not burn).

# Butternut Squash and Baked Eggs

## Makes 2 servings

Butternut squash is a starchy vegetable, so serve this dish with a green salad or with cooked greens such as spinach, chard, kale or cabbage.

## Tip

Seeds pack a great nutritional punch (especially minerals and fiber) and are somewhat lower in fats and carbs than nuts. They are also quite filling, so they make a good snack.

## NUTRIENTS PER SERVING

| | |
|---|---|
| Calories | 257 |
| Carbohydrate | 28 g |
| Fiber | 5 g |
| Protein | 9 g |
| Fat | 14 g |
| Saturated fat | 3 g |
| Cholesterol | 186 mg |
| Sodium | 81 mg |

### Food Choices

| | |
|---|---|
| 1½ | Carbohydrate |
| 1 | Meat & Alternatives |
| 2 | Fat |

- **Food processor**
- **Ovenproof casserole dish**

| | | |
|---|---|---|
| 1 tbsp | olive oil | 15 mL |
| 1 lb | butternut squash (about ½ medium), peeled and cut into large dice | 500 g |
| 1 | 1-inch (2.5 cm) piece gingerroot, peeled and cut into slivers | 1 |
| | Sea salt and freshly ground black pepper (optional) | |
| 2 | large eggs | 2 |
| 1 tbsp | unsalted sunflower seeds or green pumpkin seeds (pepitas), lightly crushed | 15 mL |

1. In a heavy pan, heat the oil over medium-low heat. Add the squash and ginger, stirring well to combine. Reduce the heat to low, cover and cook for 20 to 30 minutes or until the squash is very tender.

2. Preheat the oven to 350°F (180°C).

3. Transfer the squash mixture to the food processor and purée until smooth. Taste and season with salt and pepper, if necessary.

4. Spoon the mashed squash into the ovenproof dish. Make two hollows in the squash with the back of a spoon. Break an egg into each hollow and sprinkle liberally with the sunflower seeds.

5. Bake for 15 to 30 minutes, depending on whether you want the eggs to be soft-cooked or hard-cooked.

# Lentil and Egg Pie

### Makes 2 servings

This is quite a substantial dish, vaguely related to a moussaka but a good deal less trouble to make. It will keep for a couple of days in the fridge and reheat well in a microwave if you are on your own. Serve with a green vegetable or salad.

## Tip

Lentils are low on the glycemic index and have a low glycemic load, so they are an excellent option for people with diabetes.

### NUTRIENTS PER SERVING

| | |
|---|---|
| Calories | 478 |
| Carbohydrate | 55 g |
| Fiber | 10 g |
| Protein | 29 g |
| Fat | 14 g |
| Saturated fat | 3 g |
| Cholesterol | 189 mg |
| Sodium | 183 mg |

### Food Choices

| | |
|---|---|
| 2½ | Carbohydrate |
| 3½ | Meat & Alternatives |
| 2 | Fat |
| 2 | Extra |

• **Ovenproof casserole dish**

| | | |
|---|---|---|
| 1 tbsp | olive oil | 15 mL |
| 1 | onion, finely chopped | 1 |
| 1 | clove garlic, minced | 1 |
| 3 | drained canned anchovy fillets (optional) | 3 |
| 4 oz | mushrooms, roughly chopped | 125 g |
| ¾ cup | dried Puy or black lentils, rinsed | 175 mL |
| 1 cup | no-salt-added or reduced-sodium ready-to-use vegetable broth or miso broth | 250 mL |
| ⅓ cup | red wine (or 1 tbsp/15 mL red wine vinegar) | 75 mL |
| | Freshly ground black pepper | |
| 2 | large eggs | 2 |
| ½ cup | milk (cow's, soy or oat) | 125 mL |
| ¼ cup | chopped fresh parsley | 60 mL |

1. In a medium saucepan, heat the oil over medium heat. Cook the onion, garlic and anchovies (if using), stirring often, for 8 to 10 minutes or until the onion is softening and coloring lightly.

2. Add the mushrooms and cook for 3 to 4 minutes or until quite soft.

3. Add the lentils and cook, stirring, for 1 minute.

4. Add the broth and wine. Season with pepper to taste. Bring to a boil, then reduce the heat and simmer gently for 20 to 30 minutes or until the lentils are tender.

5. Meanwhile, preheat oven to 350°F (180°C).

6. In a bowl, beat together the eggs and milk. Stir in parsley.

7. Spoon the lentil mixture into the ovenproof dish, then pour the egg mixture over top.

8. Bake for 25 minutes or until the egg topping is set, slightly risen and browned.

# Pork, Beef and Lamb

Sausage and Bean Pot. . . . . . . . . . . . . . . . . . . . . 92

Pork Chops with Beets and Butter Beans . . . . . . . 94

Pork Medallions with Lentils and Cabbage . . . . . . 96

Pork Chops with Apple . . . . . . . . . . . . . . . . . . . . 97

Slow-Cooked Pot Roast. . . . . . . . . . . . . . . . . . . 98

Steak with Garlic . . . . . . . . . . . . . . . . . . . . . . . . 99

Beef and Mushroom Casserole . . . . . . . . . . . . . . 100

Beef Casserole with Butternut Squash . . . . . . . . 101

Coffee-Infused Beef Stew . . . . . . . . . . . . . . . . . 102

Bobotie . . . . . . . . . . . . . . . . . . . . . . . . . . . . . . 103

Beef with Curly Kale . . . . . . . . . . . . . . . . . . . . . 104

Rack of Lamb with Mustard Crust . . . . . . . . . . . 106

Lamb and Pepper Kebabs. . . . . . . . . . . . . . . . . 107

Lamb Tagine . . . . . . . . . . . . . . . . . . . . . . . . . . 108

# Sausage and Bean Pot

These kinds of one-pot meals just get better and better the longer you keep them. So if this recipe makes more than you need, store the leftovers in the fridge for 2 or 3 days. Just add a little more liquid, reheat, and you're good to go.

## Tip

In place of the red wine, you can substitute 2 tbsp (30 mL) red wine vinegar and an additional ⅓ cup (75 mL) vegetable broth.

### NUTRIENTS PER SERVING

| | |
|---|---|
| Calories | 521 |
| Carbohydrate | 64 g |
| Fiber | 14 g |
| Protein | 28 g |
| Fat | 13 g |
| Saturated fat | 3 g |
| Cholesterol | 33 mg |
| Sodium | 854 mg |

### Food Choices

| | |
|---|---|
| 2½ | Carbohydrate |
| 3½ | Meat & Alternatives |
| 2 | Fat |
| 3 | Extra |

| | | |
|---|---|---|
| 1 tbsp | olive oil | 15 mL |
| 2 | small red onions, sliced | 2 |
| 2 | cloves garlic, sliced | 2 |
| ½ | leek (white and light green parts only), trimmed and cut into thick slices | ½ |
| 1 | stalk celery, cut into thick slices | 1 |
| 4 | mushrooms, halved | 4 |
| 1 tsp | mixed dried herbs | 5 mL |
| 3 tbsp | dried Puy, green or brown lentils, rinsed | 45 mL |
| 1 tbsp | chopped dry-packed sun-dried tomatoes | 15 mL |
| 4 oz | lean pork sausage, thickly sliced | 125 g |
| ½ cup | dry red wine (see tip, at left) | 125 mL |
| 1¼ cups | no-salt-added or reduced-sodium ready-to-use vegetable broth | 300 mL |
| ¾ cup | drained rinsed canned cannellini beans (see tip, at right) | 175 mL |
| ¾ cup | drained rinsed canned borlotti beans | 175 mL |
| | Freshly ground black pepper | |
| | Chopped fresh parsley | |

1. In a heavy saucepan, heat the oil over medium-high heat. Cook the onions, garlic, leek, celery, mushrooms and herbs for 5 to 10 minutes or until very tender.

2. Add the lentils, sun-dried tomatoes, sausage, wine and broth. Bring to a boil, then reduce the heat to low, cover and simmer for 1 hour.

## Tips

If you cannot find canned cannellini and borlotti beans, try any other canned beans you can find — green beans, butter beans, flageolets, black-eyed peas, kidney beans, etc. Try to use two different types of beans, as that varies the texture and color of the bean pot. You could also cook dried beans from scratch, but that would probably (depending on the bean) involve soaking them overnight first and then boiling them until tender. They would be slightly nicer, but you may not wish to go to all that trouble.

Because there are already plenty of vegetables in the bean pot, you may not need any extras, but a fresh green salad afterwards would be good.

Thanks to the sausage and canned beans, this meal is quite high in sodium, so save it for a day when your sodium intake at other meals is low.

**3.** Add the cannellini and borlotti beans, increase heat and bring to a boil. Reduce heat to low, cover and simmer for 15 minutes. If there is too much liquid, uncover, increase the heat to medium and cook for 5 minutes to reduce the liquid. Season with lots of black pepper. Sprinkle with parsley just before serving.

## Vegetable and Chicken Broth

Ready-to-use vegetable broth and chicken broth add a tremendous amount of flavor to any number of entrées and side dishes, in addition to their use in soups. Both are now readily available in convenient Tetra Paks, which can be stored in the refrigerator for up to a week after opening, so you can use whatever amount you need for a recipe, then store the rest for the next use. Many brands now offer both reduced-sodium and no-salt-added options. When buying vegetable broth, look for one with less than 20 g of sodium per $\frac{2}{3}$ cup (150 mL). When buying chicken broth, look for one with less than 40 g of sodium per $\frac{2}{3}$ cup (150 mL).

# Pork Chops with Beets and Butter Beans

Beets and horseradish are a great combination, given an extra dimension here with the butter beans and pork chops. You can make this dish perfectly successfully for one — just halve the quantities and slightly reduce the cooking time. You do not really need another vegetable, but if you're extra-hungry, you can steam some broccoli or finish with some nice leafy greens.

| | | |
|---|---|---|
| 1 tbsp | olive oil | 15 mL |
| 2 | small boneless pork loin chops (each about 3 oz/90 g) | 2 |
| 1 | small onion, thinly sliced | 1 |
| 1 | large beet, peeled and coarsely grated | 1 |
| ¾ cup | no-salt-added or reduced-sodium ready-to-use vegetable or chicken broth | 175 mL |
| 1 cup | drained rinsed canned butter (lima) beans | 250 mL |
| 1 tbsp | prepared horseradish or grated fresh horseradish | 15 mL |
| 2 tbsp | low-fat plain yogurt (cow's, goat's, sheep's or soy) | 30 mL |
| | Juice of ½ lemon (approx.) | |
| Pinch | sea salt | Pinch |
| | Freshly ground black pepper | |

1. In a wide, heavy pan, heat the oil over medium-high heat. Cook the pork chops, turning once, for 1 to 2 minutes per side or until browned on both sides. Transfer to a plate and set aside.

2. Add the onion to the pan and cook, stirring often, for 5 minutes or until lightly browned.

3. Stir in the grated beet and broth. Return the pork chops to the pan and nestle them into the beets. Reduce heat to low, cover and simmer for 10 minutes or until beets are tender-crisp and just a hint of pink remains inside the pork.

4. Meanwhile, in a small saucepan, heat the butter beans over medium-low heat until heated through.

5. In a bowl, combine the horseradish, yogurt and lemon juice to taste. Season with a pinch of salt and with pepper to taste. Add the beans and toss to coat.

6. Serve the beans with the pork chops and beets.

## NUTRIENTS PER SERVING

| | |
|---|---|
| Calories | 321 |
| Carbohydrate | 27 g |
| Fiber | 6 g |
| Protein | 25 g |
| Fat | 13 g |
| Saturated fat | 3 g |
| Cholesterol | 46 mg |
| Sodium | 284 mg |

### Food Choices

| | |
|---|---|
| 1½ | Carbohydrate |
| 2½ | Meat & Alternatives |
| 2 | Fat |
| 2 | Extra |

# Horseradish

Fresh horseradish root is often not available and is very hard to peel and grate. However, you can buy jars of prepared horseradish, which keeps really well in the fridge. Half a teaspoon (2 mL) gives a lift to dressings and dips, is great in a sandwich and can be used to season a soup or sauce that is struggling for flavor.

# Pork Medallions with Lentils and Cabbage

Leftovers can be kept in the fridge for a couple of days, and you can use them in an omelet, a quinoa risotto or a salad, or in sandwiches with a slather of Dijon mustard or horseradish.

## Tip

Look for a chicken broth with less than 40 g of sodium per ⅔ cup (150 mL), or make your own with no added salt.

### NUTRIENTS PER SERVING

| | |
|---|---|
| Calories | 442 |
| Carbohydrate | 50 g |
| Fiber | 13 g |
| Protein | 37 g |
| Fat | 11 g |
| Saturated fat | 2 g |
| Cholesterol | 55 mg |
| Sodium | 254 mg |

### Food Choices

| | |
|---|---|
| 1½ | Carbohydrate |
| 4 | Meat & Alternatives |
| 1½ | Fat |
| 2 | Extra |

| | | |
|---|---|---|
| 6 oz | pork tenderloin, trimmed | 175 g |
| 1 tbsp | olive oil | 15 mL |
| 1 | small onion, sliced | 1 |
| 1 | large sprig fresh rosemary, leaves chopped (or 1 tsp/5 mL dried rosemary) | 1 |
| 1 tsp | coriander seeds, lightly crushed | 5 mL |
| Pinch | sea salt | Pinch |
| ½ cup | dried green lentils, rinsed | 125 mL |
| 1½ cups | no-salt-added or reduced-sodium ready-to-use chicken or vegetable broth | 375 mL |
| ½ | small green cabbage, chopped | ½ |
| | Freshly ground black pepper | |

1. In a deep pan, heat the oil over medium-high heat. Brown the pork, turning to brown all sides. Transfer to a plate and set aside.

2. Add the onion, rosemary, coriander seeds and salt to the pan. Reduce the heat to medium-low and cook, stirring often, for 5 to 10 minutes or until onion is quite soft.

3. Add the lentils and broth. Increase the heat and bring to a boil, then reduce heat to medium-low, cover and simmer for 15 minutes.

4. Add the cabbage, stirring well. Return the pork to the pan, along with with any accumulated juices, and push the pork down into the lentils. Cover and simmer for 15 to 20 minutes or until the cabbage and lentils are both very tender and just a hint of pink remains inside the pork.

5. Transfer the pork to a cutting board, tent with foil and let rest for 5 minutes. Cut into medallions and season with pepper to taste.

6. Serve pork medallions on top of the cabbage and lentil mixture.

# Pork Chops with Apple

**Makes 1 serving**

Serve with a steamed and mashed root vegetable (potato, sweet potato, celeriac or squash) and steamed broccoli or green beans.

## Tip

You can replace the wine with 1 tbsp (15 mL) white wine vinegar and 3 tbsp (45 mL) no-salt-added or reduced-sodium ready-to-use chicken or vegetable broth.

| 1 | small boneless pork chop (about 3 oz/90 g), trimmed of fat | 1 |
|---|---|---|
| 1 tsp | olive oil | 5 mL |
| 1 | small shallot, thinly sliced | 1 |
| 1/2 | small leek (white and light green parts only), trimmed and thinly sliced | 1/2 |
| 1/2 | small tart cooking apple (unpeeled), finely chopped | 1/2 |
| 1/4 cup | dry white wine (see tip, at left) | 60 mL |
| 1 | sprig fresh rosemary, leaves chopped (or 1/2 tsp/2 mL dried rosemary) | 1 |
| Pinch | Sea salt | Pinch |
| | Coarsely ground black pepper | |

1. In a small skillet, heat olive oil over medium-low heat. Add the shallot, leek and apple, cover and cook for 10 to 15 minutes or until very soft.

2. Stir in the wine and rosemary, then lay the pork chop on top. Season with a pinch of salt and pepper. Cover and cook for 30 minutes, or until just a hint of pink remains inside the pork.

## NUTRIENTS PER SERVING

| | |
|---|---|
| Calories | 267 |
| Carbohydrate | 18 g |
| Fiber | 3 g |
| Protein | 18 g |
| Fat | 9 g |
| Saturated fat | 2 g |
| Cholesterol | 45 mg |
| Sodium | 227 mg |

### Food Choices

| | |
|---|---|
| 1/2 | Carbohydrate |
| 2 1/2 | Meat & Alternatives |
| 1 | Fat |
| 1 | Extra |

## Stewed or Baked Apple

When you find yourself with half an apple left over, stew it with a little water and a few raisins (no extra sugar needed) and eat it for breakfast. Or mix some raisins with a few nuts (almonds, walnuts or cashews), pile them in a mound in an ovenproof casserole dish, sit the apple on top of the nuts and add a little water to the dish. Cover and bake in a preheated 350°F (180°C) oven for 30 minutes. Eat as a dessert.

# Slow-Cooked Pot Roast

This roast will be much larger than you need for one meal, but the leftovers make really delicious cold beef for a salad or sandwiches. Serve with baked potatoes and a green vegetable.

## Tip

In place of the red wine, you can substitute 2 tbsp (30 mL) red wine vinegar or balsamic vinegar and ½ cup (125 mL) no-salt-added or reduced-sodium ready-to-use beef broth.

### NUTRIENTS PER 1 OF 6 SERVINGS

| | |
|---|---|
| Calories | 358 |
| Carbohydrate | 8 g |
| Fiber | 2 g |
| Protein | 20 g |
| Fat | 25 g |
| Saturated fat | 10 g |
| Cholesterol | 82 mg |
| Sodium | 234 mg |

### Food Choices

| | |
|---|---|
| 2½ | Meat & Alternatives |
| 3½ | Fat |
| 1 | Extra |

- **Preheat oven to 300°F (150°C)**
- **Heavy casserole dish**

| | | |
|---|---|---|
| 1½ lbs | boneless beef chuck, cross rib or blade roast | 750 g |
| 4 | small onions, peeled but left whole | 4 |
| 4 | cloves garlic, peeled but left whole | 4 |
| 4 | mushrooms | 4 |
| 2 | carrots, cut in half | 2 |
| 4 | bay leaves | 4 |
| 1 tsp | whole black peppercorns | 5 mL |
| ⅔ cup | dry red wine (see tip, at left) | 150 mL |
| | Water | |
| 6 | black olives | 6 |
| ¼ tsp | sea salt | 1 mL |
| | Freshly ground black pepper | |

1. Place the roast in a heavy casserole dish that holds it fairly snugly. Surround it with the onions, garlic, mushrooms and carrots. Add the bay leaves, peppercorns and wine, then add water until the meat is covered.

2. Cover and bake in preheated oven for 2 to 4 hours or until cooked to desired doneness.

3. Allow the meat to cool in the juices, then chill until any fat solidifies on top. Remove the fat and gently reheat the roast. Add the olives and season the juices with salt and with pepper to taste.

# Steak with Garlic

If you are on your own and feel like a treat, try this dish! The preparation is incredibly simple, but will improve even the best cut of steak.

## Tip

Serve with a baked potato and a green vegetable or salad. Or, if you don't want to heat the oven for just one potato, serve your steak on a thick slice of really nice whole-grain bread, which will absorb its juices so that they aren't wasted.

• **Baking sheet (optional)**

| | | |
|---|---|---|
| 4 oz | piece trimmed boneless grilling steak (strip loin, tenderloin or top sirloin) | 125 g |
| Pinch | sea salt | Pinch |
| | Freshly ground black pepper | |
| 4 | cloves garlic | 4 |

1. Lay the steak out on a plate and grate salt and a little black pepper over top.

2. Crush 2 cloves of garlic in a garlic press and spread over the steak.

3. Turn the steak and repeat the process on the other side. Cover and refrigerate for 1 to 2 hours to absorb the flavors.

4. Preheat the barbecue grill to medium or preheat the broiler. If using the broiler, place the steak on a baking sheet. Grill or broil the steak, turning once, until cooked to desired doneness.

## NUTRIENTS PER SERVING

| | |
|---|---|
| Calories | 174 |
| Carbohydrate | 4 g |
| Fiber | 0 g |
| Protein | 27 g |
| Fat | 6 g |
| Saturated fat | 2 g |
| Cholesterol | 71 mg |
| Sodium | 242 mg |

### Food Choices

| | |
|---|---|
| 3½ | Meat & Alternatives |
| 1 | Extra |

# Beef and Mushroom Casserole

## Tips

To make a bouquet garni, tie together sprigs of fresh herbs (such as thyme, bay leaf, parsley, rosemary, sage, etc.) or place them in a cheesecloth bag. If fresh herbs are not available, use a mixture of dried herbs tied in cheesecloth or placed in a tea infuser.

Thanks to the anchovies, this meal is very high in sodium, so save it for a day when your sodium intake at other meals is low.

### NUTRIENTS PER SERVING

| | |
|---|---|
| Calories | 448 |
| Carbohydrate | 12 g |
| Fiber | 2 g |
| Protein | 39 g |
| Fat | 23 g |
| Saturated fat | 5 g |
| Cholesterol | 108 mg |
| Sodium | 1699 mg |

### Food Choices

| | |
|---|---|
| 5 | Meat & Alternatives |
| 2½ | Fat |
| 2 | Extra |

| | | |
|---|---|---|
| 2 tbsp | olive oil | 30 mL |
| 2 | drained canned anchovies, chopped | 2 |
| 2 | onions, thickly sliced | 2 |
| 8 oz | stewing beef, trimmed and cubed | 250 g |
| 1 tbsp | whole wheat flour | 15 mL |
| 6 tbsp | robust red wine | 90 mL |
| ¾ cup | water | 175 mL |
| 4 oz | mushrooms, roughly chopped | 125 g |
| | Bouquet garni (see tip, at left) | |
| 4 | whole black peppercorns | 4 |

1. In a heavy saucepan, heat the oil over medium-high heat. Cook the anchovies and onions, stirring often, until they start to turn color.

2. Add the beef and cook, stirring often, until well browned on all sides. Add the flour and cook, stirring, for 1 minute.

3. Gradually add the wine, scraping up any browned bits from the bottom of the pan.

4. Stir in the water, mushrooms, bouquet garni and peppercorns. Bring to a boil, then reduce heat to low, cover and simmer for 30 to 45 minutes or until the beef is fork-tender. Discard the bouquet garni before serving.

# Beef Casserole with Butternut Squash

This all-in-one dish not only tastes warming but looks it too. The casserole freezes well, so, if you want to double up on the quantities, you could freeze half for a future occasion.

## Tip

In place of the red wine, you can substitute 2 tbsp (30 mL) red wine vinegar and 1/3 cup (75 mL) no-salt-added or reduced-sodium ready-to-use beef broth.

| NUTRIENTS PER SERVING | |
|---|---|
| Calories | 338 |
| Carbohydrate | 19 g |
| Fiber | 3 g |
| Protein | 25 g |
| Fat | 14 g |
| Saturated fat | 3 g |
| Cholesterol | 65 mg |
| Sodium | 254 mg |
| **Food Choices** | |
| 3 | Meat & Alternatives |
| 1 | Fat |
| 2 | Extra |

| | | |
|---|---|---|
| 1 tbsp | olive oil | 15 mL |
| 1 | 1-inch (2.5 cm) piece gingerroot, cut into thin strips | 1 |
| 2 | shallots or very small onions, peeled | 2 |
| 1 | small butternut squash, peeled and cut into medium-size cubes | 1 |
| 1 tbsp | all-purpose flour | 15 mL |
| 1/8 tsp | sea salt | 0.5 mL |
| | Freshly ground black pepper | |
| 8 oz | stewing beef, trimmed and cubed | 250 g |
| 1/2 cup | red wine or Marsala | 125 mL |
| 2/3 cup | water | 150 mL |
| 2 | bay leaves | 2 |

1. In a heavy saucepan, heat the oil over medium heat. Cook the ginger and shallots, stirring often, until softened.
2. Add the squash, increase heat to medium-high and cook, stirring often, until lightly browned on all sides.
3. Meanwhile, season the flour with salt and pepper. Add the beef and toss to coat.
4. Add the beef to the pot and cook, stirring often, for 3 to 4 minutes or until well browned on all sides.
5. Gradually add the wine, scraping up any browned bits from the bottom of the pot.
6. Stir in the water and bay leaves. Bring to a boil, stirring constantly until the sauce is slightly thickened. Reduce the heat and simmer for 45 to 60 minutes or until the beef and squash are fork-tender.

# Coffee-Infused Beef Stew

This stew's sauce has a lovely smoky flavor that's definitely exotic! Serve with brown rice or baked potatoes and a green vegetable.

## Tip

Although there is some dispute over whether coffee has a positive effect on blood sugar, it certainly does not have a negative one. In any case, the small amount in this dish is scarcely likely to affect you one way or the other.

| | | |
|---|---|---|
| 1 | slice bacon, chopped | 1 |
| 2 | cloves garlic, finely chopped or crushed | 2 |
| 12 oz | stewing beef, trimmed and cubed | 375 g |
| 1 | small red bell pepper, chopped | 1 |
| 1 cup | canned tomatoes, with a little of the juice drained off | 250 mL |
| ¼ cup | strong brewed black coffee | 60 mL |
| ¼ cup | red wine | 60 mL |
| 1 oz | dark chocolate, grated | 30 g |
| | Freshly ground black pepper | |

1. In a heavy saucepan, cook the chopped bacon and garlic over medium heat, stirring often, until lightly browned.

2. Add the beef, increase the heat to medium-high and cook, stirring often, until browned on all sides.

3. Add the red pepper, reduce the heat to medium and cook, stirring often, for 2 to 3 minutes or until beginning to soften.

4. Stir in the tomatoes, coffee, wine and chocolate. Reduce the heat to low, cover and simmer for 30 to 45 minutes or until the beef is fork-tender. Season with pepper to taste.

## NUTRIENTS PER SERVING

| | |
|---|---|
| Calories | 450 |
| Carbohydrate | 19 g |
| Fiber | 4 g |
| Protein | 40 g |
| Fat | 20 g |
| Saturated fat | 8 g |
| Cholesterol | 107 mg |
| Sodium | 479 mg |

### Food Choices

| | |
|---|---|
| ½ | Carbohydrate |
| 5 | Meat & Alternatives |
| 2 | Fat |
| 2 | Extra |

# Bobotie

Bobotie is a traditional South African dish that resembles a spicy moussaka, although with a more interesting blend of flavors. If you have any left over, it also tastes good cold. Serve with cooked brown rice or quinoa, homemade chutney and a green salad.

## Tip

Choose a mild, medium or hot curry powder according to your taste and how spicy you'd like your bobotie.

### NUTRIENTS PER SERVING

| | |
|---|---|
| Calories | 466 |
| Carbohydrate | 30 g |
| Fiber | 3 g |
| Protein | 40 g |
| Fat | 21 g |
| Saturated fat | 6 g |
| Cholesterol | 258 mg |
| Sodium | 395 mg |

### Food Choices

| | |
|---|---|
| 1½ | Carbohydrate |
| 4 | Meat & Alternatives |
| 1½ | Fat |
| 2 | Extra |

- **Preheat oven to 350°F (180°C)**
- **Food processor**
- **Ovenproof casserole dish**

| | | |
|---|---|---|
| 1 | thick slice whole-grain bread | 1 |
| 2 cups | milk, divided | 500 mL |
| 8 oz | extra-lean ground beef | 250 g |
| 1 tbsp | olive oil | 15 mL |
| 1 | onion, finely chopped | 1 |
| 1 tbsp | curry powder (see tip, at left) | 15 mL |
| ½ tsp | packed dark brown sugar | 2 mL |
| ¼ tsp | freshly ground black pepper | 1 mL |
| Pinch | sea salt | Pinch |
| 2 | large eggs, lightly beaten | 2 |
| | Juice of 2 small lemons | |
| 1 tbsp | toasted chopped unsalted almonds or cashews | 15 mL |
| 1 tbsp | raisins | 15 mL |

1. Place the bread in a bowl and pour half of the milk over top. Soak for 5 minutes.

2. Transfer the bread to the food processor, add the beef and pulse until minced. Set aside.

3. In a small frying pan, heat the oil over medium heat. Cook the onion and curry powder, stirring often, until lightly browned. Remove from heat and set aside.

4. In a large bowl, combine brown sugar, pepper, salt, one egg and lemon juice. Stir in the onion mixture. Add the beef mixture and mix until well combined. Spoon into the casserole dish.

5. In a small bowl, combine the remaining milk, the remaining egg, the almonds and the raisins. Pour over the beef mixture, allowing the liquid to soak in and making sure the fruit and nuts are well distributed over the top.

6. Bake in preheated oven, uncovered, for 30 minutes or until the top is lightly browned and puffed.

# Beef with Curly Kale

This rich and spicy all-in-one-pot meal is yet another dish that benefits from being cooked in advance and left overnight to allow its flavors to mature. There are so many vegetables already in the dish that you should not need any extras.

| | | |
|---|---|---|
| 1 tbsp | olive oil | 15 mL |
| 1 | red onion, chopped | 1 |
| 1 | clove garlic, sliced | 1 |
| 1 | carrot, sliced | 1 |
| ½ | red bell pepper, cut into large squares | ½ |
| 1 | small hot green chile pepper, seeded and finely chopped | 1 |
| 3 oz | small mushrooms, halved | 90 g |
| 1 cup | chopped celery root | 250 mL |
| 1 tsp | dried thyme | 5 mL |
| 6 oz | extra-lean ground beef | 175 g |
| 1 | can (14 oz/398 mL) no-salt-added diced tomatoes, with juice (or 1½ cups/375 mL) | 1 |
| 2 tbsp | red wine (or 2 tsp/10 mL red wine vinegar) | 30 mL |
| | Freshly ground black pepper | |
| 1 cup | drained rinsed canned beans (any type) | 250 mL |
| 4 cups | packed trimmed curly kale, chopped | 1 L |

## NUTRIENTS PER SERVING

| | |
|---|---|
| Calories | 471 |
| Carbohydrate | 59 g |
| Fiber | 15 g |
| Protein | 32 g |
| Fat | 13 g |
| Saturated fat | 2 g |
| Cholesterol | 45 mg |
| Sodium | 299 mg |

### Food Choices

| | |
|---|---|
| 3 | Carbohydrate |
| 3 | Meat & Alternatives |
| 1½ | Fat |
| 2 | Extra |

1. In a large saucepan, heat the oil over medium heat. Cook the onion and garlic, stirring often, until slightly softened.

2. Add the carrot, red pepper, chile pepper and mushrooms. Cook, stirring often, for 2 minutes.

3. Add the celery root, thyme and beef. Cook, breaking the beef up with a spoon, until no longer pink.

4. Stir in the tomatoes and wine. Season with pepper to taste. Bring to a boil, then reduce the heat to low, cover and simmer for 40 minutes.

5. Stir in the beans and kale. Cook for 10 minutes or until the kale is tender.

Fillet of Cod with Chiles (page 60)

Moules Marinières (page 69)

Stir-Fried Shrimp with Ginger (page 70)

Herb Frittata (page 86)

Steak with Garlic (page 99)

Whole Wheat Blueberry Muffins (page 114)

Old-Fashioned Ginger and
Honey Cookies (page 115)

Pears with Chocolate and Ginger Wine Sauce (page 133)

Hot Fruit Salad (page 134)

Coconut Milk Crème (page 136)

Chocolate Strawberries (page 139)

# Curly Kale

Curly kale is a bit of an acquired taste, as it is quite strong — although it can be tamed by other strong flavors, as in Beef with Curly Kale. It is strongly anti-inflammatory, has a very low glycemic load, is very high in vitamins A, C and K, and is a reasonable source of manganese, potassium and copper.

# Rack of Lamb with Mustard Crust

**Makes 2 servings**

A rack of lamb is perfect for a small number of people, as you can get as few or as many cutlets on it as you need. However, you must be careful not to let it dry out — which is why cooking it over the potatoes is a good idea.

- **Preheat oven to 350°F (180°C)**
- **Small, heavy ovenproof pot**

| | | |
|---|---|---|
| 1 tbsp | olive oil | 15 mL |
| 1 | leek (white and light green parts only), trimmed and thickly sliced | 1 |
| 1 | slice bacon, roughly chopped | 1 |
| 2 | potatoes, thinly sliced | 2 |
| 2 tbsp | fresh whole wheat bread crumbs | 30 mL |
| 1 tbsp | Dijon mustard | 15 mL |
| 1 | small rack of lamb | 1 |
| 2 | sprigs fresh rosemary (or ½ tsp/2 mL dried) | 2 |
| 2 | sprigs fresh thyme (or ½ tsp/2 mL dried) | 2 |

1. In a small, heavy ovenproof pot large enough to hold the lamb, heat the oil over medium-high heat. Cook the leek and bacon, stirring often, until lightly browned.

2. Add the potatoes, reduce the heat to medium and cook, stirring often, for 5 minutes.

3. Meanwhile, in a bowl, combine the bread crumbs and mustard. Spread the mixture over the lamb.

4. Lay the rosemary and thyme sprigs (or sprinkle the dried herbs) over the potatoes. Lay the lamb on top of the potatoes, skin side up.

5. Cover the pot tightly, transfer to the preheated oven and bake for 20 minutes or until the lamb is cooked to desired doneness.

**NUTRIENTS PER SERVING**

| | |
|---|---|
| Calories | 482 |
| Carbohydrate | 50 g |
| Fiber | 6 g |
| Protein | 24 g |
| Fat | 20 g |
| Saturated fat | 6 g |
| Cholesterol | 64 mg |
| Sodium | 408 mg |

**Food Choices**

| | |
|---|---|
| 2½ | Carbohydrate |
| 2½ | Meat & Alternatives |
| 2½ | Fat |
| 3 | Extra |

# Lamb and Pepper Kebabs

Kebabs are great for small numbers, as you only have to make as many as you need. Although it is fun to cook them on the barbecue, they taste 99% as good when cooked under the broiler. Serve with whole-grain pita bread and a green salad.

- **Two 12-inch (30 cm) wooden skewers**
- **Baking sheet (optional)**

| | | |
|---|---|---|
| 4 | green onions, finely chopped | 4 |
| 1 | small clove garlic, crushed | 1 |
| 2 tbsp | minced gingerroot | 30 mL |
| 1 tsp | ground turmeric | 5 mL |
| | Juice of 1 small lemon | |
| 1 tbsp | plain yogurt (cow's, goat's, sheep's or soy) | 15 mL |
| 1 tbsp | sesame, nut or olive oil | 15 mL |
| 1 tsp | reduced-sodium soy sauce | 5 mL |
| 7 oz | boneless lamb loin or leg (or beef sirloin), trimmed and cut into 1½-inch (3 cm) chunks | 210 g |
| 1 | yellow bell pepper, cut into large squares | 1 |
| 1 | zucchini, cut into thick rounds | 1 |
| | Freshly ground black pepper | |

1. In a large bowl, combine the green onions, garlic, ginger, turmeric, lemon juice, yogurt, oil and soy sauce. Add the lamb and toss to coat. Cover and refrigerate for at least 4 hours or overnight.

2. Preheat the barbecue grill to medium or preheat the broiler. Soak the skewers in water for 15 minutes.

3. Remove the lamb from the marinade, discarding marinade. Thread lamb onto skewers alternately with the yellow pepper and zucchini. Season lightly with pepper. If using the broiler, place skewers on the baking sheet.

4. Grill skewers on the barbecue or under the broiler, turning occasionally, for 5 to 7 minutes or until browned on all sides and cooked to desired doneness.

## NUTRIENTS PER SERVING

| | |
|---|---|
| Calories | 258 |
| Carbohydrate | 11 g |
| Fiber | 2 g |
| Protein | 23 g |
| Fat | 13 g |
| Saturated fat | 3 g |
| Cholesterol | 66 mg |
| Sodium | 178 mg |

### Food Choices

| | |
|---|---|
| 3 | Meat & Alternatives |
| 1½ | Fat |
| 5 | Extra |

# Lamb Tagine

A tagine is a slow-cooked North African stew, originally cooked over an open fire in one of those wonderful tall-lidded earthenware pots. Because of the complex mix of flavors, it really benefits from the long, slow cooking and is often better on day two than day one, so don't worry if this recipe makes more than you need for a single meal. Serve the tagine alone or with whole-grain pita bread or flatbread.

| | | |
|---|---|---|
| 1 tbsp | olive oil | 15 mL |
| 1 | small onion, thinly sliced | 1 |
| 1 | carrot, sliced | 1 |
| 1 | stalk celery, finely chopped | 1 |
| 1 to 2 | large cloves garlic, sliced | 1 to 2 |
| 2 tsp | ground cumin | 10 mL |
| 1 tsp | ground coriander | 5 mL |
| 8 oz | lean boneless lamb stewing meat | 250 g |
| ½ | eggplant, halved lengthways and sliced | ½ |
| 2 | dried limes (see tip, at right) | 2 |
| | Grated zest of ¼ lemon | |
| 1 cup | chopped fresh or drained canned tomatoes | 250 mL |
| ¾ cup | no-salt-added or reduced-sodium ready-to-use vegetable broth | 175 mL |
| 2 cups | packed fresh spinach, roughly chopped | 500 mL |
| 1 cup | drained rinsed canned or cooked chickpeas | 250 mL |
| | Freshly ground black pepper | |
| | Chopped fresh cilantro | |
| 2 tsp | harissa (or to taste) | 10 mL |

1. In a heavy pan (preferably cast-iron), heat the oil over medium-high heat. Cook the onion, carrot, celery, garlic, cumin and coriander, stirring often, for 4 to 5 minutes or until the vegetables are starting to soften.

2. Add the lamb and cook, stirring often, for 3 to 4 minutes or until browned on all sides.

## NUTRIENTS PER SERVING

| | |
|---|---|
| Calories | 470 |
| Carbohydrate | 49 g |
| Fiber | 16 g |
| Protein | 33 g |
| Fat | 17 g |
| Saturated fat | 4 g |
| Cholesterol | 73 mg |
| Sodium | 426 mg |

### Food Choices

| | |
|---|---|
| 1 | Carbohydrate |
| 4 | Meat & Alternatives |
| 2 | Fat |
| 6 | Extra |

## Tips

Look for dried limes in Middle Eastern specialty stores or in large, well-stocked supermarkets.

Look for a vegetable broth with less than 20 g of sodium per $\frac{2}{3}$ cup (150 mL), or make your own with no added salt.

Start with no more than 1 tsp (5 mL) harissa per serving; it can be quite hot and may overpower the lamb if you use too much.

3. Stir in the eggplant, limes, lemon zest, tomatoes and broth. Bring to a boil, then reduce the heat to low, cover and simmer for $1\frac{1}{2}$ hours.

4. Add the chickpeas and spinach. Season to taste with pepper. Return to a simmer and simmer for 45 minutes.

5. Stir in the cilantro and serve the tagine with harissa.

## Harissa

Harissa is a classic North African condiment found on every table in Tunisia and Algeria, and on most in Morocco. It is also used as an ingredient in stews and as a rub for meats and eggplant.

There are as many recipes for harissa as there are families who make it, but the main ingredients are hot chile peppers and olive oil. Harissa may also include red bell peppers, garlic, cumin, coriander and lemon juice, and in some regions can taste quite smoky.

It is worth buying a good-quality harissa, as the flavor will be more complex and interesting — rather than just hot — and it will last a long time. It can be used in all kinds of non-African dishes, too; try it on pasta or pizza, or even in sandwiches.

# Baked Goods and Desserts

Banana and Polenta Bread . . . . . . . . . . . . . . 112

Whole Wheat Blueberry Muffins . . . . . . . . . . . . 114

Old-Fashioned Ginger and Honey Cookies . . . . . 115

Lemon Shortbread . . . . . . . . . . . . . . . . . . . 116

Cinnamon Oat Squares . . . . . . . . . . . . . . . . 117

Chocolate Brownies . . . . . . . . . . . . . . . . . . 118

Baked Lemon and Almond Cheesecake . . . . . . . 119

Chocolate Plum Cake . . . . . . . . . . . . . . . . . 120

Rich Seedy Cake . . . . . . . . . . . . . . . . . . . . 121

Lemon Poppy Seed Cake . . . . . . . . . . . . . . . 122

Upside-Down Fruitcake . . . . . . . . . . . . . . . . 124

Seriously Nutty Fruitcake . . . . . . . . . . . . . . . 126

Strawberry Oat Crumble . . . . . . . . . . . . . . . 128

Apple Berry Crumble . . . . . . . . . . . . . . . . . 130

Hot Plum Dessert . . . . . . . . . . . . . . . . . . . 131

Apple and Cranberry Clafouti . . . . . . . . . . . . 132

Pears with Chocolate and Ginger Wine Sauce . . . 133

Hot Fruit Salad . . . . . . . . . . . . . . . . . . . . . 134

Coconut Milk Crème . . . . . . . . . . . . . . . . . 136

Chocolate Pots . . . . . . . . . . . . . . . . . . . . . 138

Chocolate Strawberries . . . . . . . . . . . . . . . . 139

# Banana and Polenta Bread

This incredibly easy recipe makes one small loaf that freezes well. I do not add any sugar to the loaf, so it ends up as a cross between bread and cake — good either on its own or with butter.

- **Preheat oven to 350°F (180°C)**
- **Food processor**
- **8- by 4-inch (20 by 10 cm) loaf pan, bottom lined with parchment paper and sides greased**

| | | |
|---|---|---|
| 2 | ripe bananas | 2 |
| 1 cup | coarse cornmeal | 250 mL |
| 2½ tsp | baking powder | 12 mL |
| Pinch | salt | Pinch |
| 1 | large egg | 1 |
| 6 tbsp | milk | 90 mL |
| ¼ cup | butter, margarine or coconut oil | 60 mL |

1. In the food processor, purée the bananas until smooth. Add cornmeal, baking powder, salt, egg, milk and butter, and process until smooth. Spoon into the prepared pan.

2. Bake in preheated oven for 35 minutes or until a tester inserted in the center comes out clean.

3. Remove the loaf from the oven and let it cool slightly on a wire cooling rack. Turn the loaf out of the pan onto the rack, cover with a clean tea towel and let cool completely.

## NUTRIENTS PER SLICE

| | |
|---|---|
| Calories | 120 |
| Carbohydrate | 15 g |
| Fiber | 3 g |
| Protein | 2 g |
| Fat | 6 g |
| Saturated fat | 3 g |
| Cholesterol | 32 mg |
| Sodium | 148 mg |

### Food Choices

| | |
|---|---|
| 1 | Carbohydrate |
| 1 | Fat |

# Bananas

The glycemic index and glycemic load of bananas varies depending on how ripe they are, because much of the carbohydrate in green or under-ripe bananas is in the form of a resistant starch that we cannot digest. As the banana ripens, the starch is converted into sugar. Nonetheless, because of their large amount of fiber, even ripe bananas, which average around 50 on the glycemic index, are okay for people with diabetes.

# Whole Wheat Blueberry Muffins

Muffins are always good for that Sunday-morning-with-the-papers breakfast. If you want to keep some for next weekend, you can freeze two successfully. Allow them to thaw slowly at room temperature — they won't take long.

- Preheat oven to 350°F (180°C)
- Muffin pan, 3 to 4 cups lined with paper liners or greased

| | | |
|---|---|---|
| 2 tbsp | demerara sugar | 30 mL |
| 2 tbsp | butter, softened, or coconut oil | 30 mL |
| 1 | small egg (or 2 tbsp/30 mL beaten egg) | 1 |
| ¼ cup | milk or buttermilk | 60 mL |
| ½ cup | whole wheat flour | 125 mL |
| ¾ tsp | baking powder | 3 mL |
| Pinch | salt | Pinch |
| ⅓ cup | blueberries | 75 mL |

1. In a large bowl, using an electric mixer or a wooden spoon, beat the sugar, butter, egg and milk.

2. In a small bowl, whisk together the flour, baking powder and salt.

3. Gradually beat the flour mixture into the liquid mixture. Fold in the blueberries. Spoon the batter into the prepared muffin pan. Fill the empty muffin cups with water.

4. Bake in preheated oven for 20 minutes or until a tester inserted in the center of a muffin comes out clean.

5. Remove the muffins from the oven and let them cool slightly on a wire cooling rack. Serve warm or transfer to the wire rack to cool completely.

## NUTRIENTS PER MUFFIN

| | |
|---|---|
| Calories | 150 |
| Carbohydrate | 18 g |
| Fiber | 2 g |
| Protein | 4 g |
| Fat | 7 g |
| Saturated fat | 4 g |
| Cholesterol | 51 mg |
| Sodium | 169 mg |

### Food Choices

| | |
|---|---|
| 1 | Carbohydrate |
| 1 | Fat |

# Old-Fashioned Ginger and Honey Cookies

**Makes 8 cookies**

If you want to make gingerbread men, use a gingerbread man cookie cutter and give each cookie a face: place two currants for the eyes and a raisin for the nose, and draw in the mouth with the tip of a knife.

## Tip

Make sure to give the dough enough time to chill. If you try to roll it out too soon it will be too soft to handle.

### NUTRIENTS PER COOKIE

| | |
|---|---|
| Calories | 131 |
| Carbohydrate | 21 g |
| Fiber | 0 g |
| Protein | 2 g |
| Fat | 5 g |
| Saturated fat | 3 g |
| Cholesterol | 11 mg |
| Sodium | 40 mg |

**Food Choices**

| | |
|---|---|
| 1 | Carbohydrate |
| 1 | Fat |

- Cookie cutter (optional)
- Baking sheet

| | | |
|---|---|---|
| 1 cup | sifted all-purpose flour | 250 mL |
| ½ tsp | ground ginger | 2 mL |
| 3 tbsp | packed dark brown sugar | 45 mL |
| | Grated zest of 1 orange | |
| | Grated zest of 1 lemon | |
| 3 tbsp | butter, melted | 45 mL |
| 2 tbsp | liquid honey, melted | 30 mL |

1. In a small bowl, combine the flour, ginger, brown sugar, orange zest and lemon zest.

2. In a medium bowl, combine the butter and honey. Add the dry ingredients and mix to a stiff paste. Cover and refrigerate for several hours or overnight.

3. Preheat the oven to 350°F (180°C).

4. On a lightly floured work surface, roll out the dough to ¼-inch (0.5 cm) thickness. Using the cookie cutter or a knife, cut out 8 cookies, rerolling scraps as necessary. Place cookies about 2 inches (5 cm) apart on the baking sheet.

5. Bake in preheated oven for 12 to 15 minutes or until lightly browned.

6. Remove the cookies from the oven and let them cool on the pan on a wire cooling rack for 3 minutes. Transfer the cookies to the rack to cool completely.

# Lemon Shortbread

These cookies are lovely with a cup of coffee or tea. Although you are using pure sugar, the blood glucose boost will be at least partly counteracted by the acidity of the lemon zest.

- **Preheat oven to 325°F (160°C)**
- **Small baking pan or baking sheet**

| | | |
|---|---|---|
| 2 tbsp | butter, softened, or coconut oil | 30 mL |
| 3 tbsp | pale muscovado sugar | 45 mL |
| | Grated zest of 1 small lemon | |
| 6 tbsp | all-purpose flour | 90 mL |
| ¼ cup | ground almonds | 60 mL |

1. In a medium bowl, using an electric mixer or a wooden spoon, beat the butter, sugar and lemon zest until soft and light.

2. Using your fingers, rub in the flour and ground almonds, working as lightly as you can.

3. Pat the mixture out into the bottom of the baking pan, or shape it into a round about 8 inches (20 cm) in diameter and place it on the baking sheet.

4. Bake in preheated oven for 15 minutes. Remove from the oven and, using a knife, score into 6 wedges. Return to the oven and bake for 5 minutes.

5. Remove the pan from the oven to a wire cooling rack and let cool slightly. Cut into 6 wedges along the score marks. Using a spatula, carefully transfer the wedges to the rack to cool completely.

**NUTRIENTS PER COOKIE**

| | |
|---|---|
| Calories | 108 |
| Carbohydrate | 13 g |
| Fiber | 0 g |
| Protein | 2 g |
| Fat | 6 g |
| Saturated fat | 3 g |
| Cholesterol | 10 mg |
| Sodium | 34 mg |

**Food Choices**

| | |
|---|---|
| 1 | Carbohydrate |
| 1 | Fat |

# Cinnamon Oat Squares

**Makes 6 squares**

You can convert these into ginger oat squares, if you prefer, by substituting ground ginger for the cinnamon in the recipe. The seeds give a really interesting texture to the squares.

## Tip

The crumbs that inevitably fall from the squares as you transfer them to the rack are delicious sprinkled over yogurt.

- **Preheat the oven to 350°F (180°C)**
- **Small baking pan or ovenproof flan dish**

| ¼ cup | butter, margarine or coconut oil | 60 mL |
|---|---|---|
| 1 tbsp | agave syrup, pure maple syrup, liquid honey or dark (cooking) molasses | 15 mL |
| ¾ cup | quick-cooking rolled oats | 175 mL |
| 1 tbsp | whole wheat flour | 15 mL |
| ¾ tsp | ground cinnamon | 3 mL |
| 1 tbsp | unsalted sunflower seeds or green pumpkin seeds (pepitas), chopped | 15 mL |

1. In a small saucepan, melt the butter and agave syrup over medium-low heat. Cook, stirring, for 1 minute.

2. Remove from the heat and stir in oats, flour, cinnamon and sunflower seeds until a sticky dough forms.

3. Using your fingers, press the dough out into the bottom of the baking pan or flan dish (wooden spoons will just stick to it). It should be about ½ inch (1 cm) deep (the thickness of your thumb).

4. Bake in preheated oven for 18 to 20 minutes or until lightly browned.

5. Remove from the oven and, using a knife, cut the mixture into 6 squares or wedges (depending on the shape of your dish).

6. Let cool slightly in the pan on a wire cooling rack, then use a spatula or a flexible knife to carefully lever the squares out of the pan and transfer them to the rack to cool completely.

## NUTRIENTS PER SQUARE

| | |
|---|---|
| Calories | 129 |
| Carbohydrate | 11 g |
| Fiber | 1 g |
| Protein | 2 g |
| Fat | 9 g |
| Saturated fat | 5 g |
| Cholesterol | 26 mg |
| Sodium | 68 mg |

### Food Choices

| ½ | Carbohydrate |
|---|---|
| 1½ | Fat |

# Chocolate Brownies

**Makes
12 brownies**

Brownies are a classic comfort food . . . what more needs to be said?

- Preheat the oven to 325°F (160°C)
- Mini chopper or food processor
- Square or rectangular baking pan, well greased

| | | |
|---|---|---|
| ¾ cup | quick-cooking rolled oats | 175 mL |
| ⅔ cup | sifted chickpea (gram) flour | 150 mL |
| ½ cup | buckwheat flour | 125 mL |
| 1 tbsp | baking powder | 15 mL |
| ⅔ cup | reduced-fat margarine | 150 mL |
| ⅔ cup | dark muscovado sugar | 150 mL |
| ⅔ cup | unsweetened cocoa powder | 150 mL |
| ½ cup | milk | 125 mL |
| ½ cup | chopped walnuts | 125 mL |

1. In the mini chopper or food processor, process oats to a coarse powder.

2. In a small bowl, whisk together the oat powder, chickpea flour, buckwheat flour and baking powder. Set aside.

3. In a large bowl, using an electric mixer, beat the margarine, sugar and cocoa until light and fluffy.

4. With the mixer on low speed, alternately beat in the flour mixture and the milk, making three additions of flour and two of milk and beating until just blended.

5. Using a spatula, fold in the walnuts. Spoon the mixture into the prepared pan and smooth the top with the spatula.

6. Bake in preheated oven for 30 minutes or until a tester inserted in the center comes out clean.

7. Remove the pan from the oven and let cool slightly on a wire cooling rack. Using a knife, cut the cake into 8 squares. Use a spatula or a flexible knife to carefully lever the squares out of the pan and transfer them to the rack to cool completely.

## NUTRIENTS PER BROWNIE

| | |
|---|---|
| Calories | 180 |
| Carbohydrate | 22 g |
| Fiber | 3 g |
| Protein | 4 g |
| Fat | 10 g |
| Saturated fat | 2 g |
| Cholesterol | 1 mg |
| Sodium | 164 mg |

### Food Choices

| | |
|---|---|
| 1 | Carbohydrate |
| 1½ | Fat |

# Baked Lemon and Almond Cheesecake

Cheesecake keeps well, so make enough for two even if you are on your own.

## Tip

Lemon juice is good for people with diabetes, as it improves digestion and therefore the efficiency with which you digest carbohydrates.

| NUTRIENTS PER SERVING | |
|---|---|
| Calories | 207 |
| Carbohydrate | 18 g |
| Fiber | 1 g |
| Protein | 16 g |
| Fat | 9 g |
| Saturated fat | 2 g |
| Cholesterol | 103 mg |
| Sodium | 221 mg |
| **Food Choices** | |
| 1 | Carbohydrate |
| 2 | Meat & Alternatives |
| ½ | Extra |

- **Preheat oven to 300°F (150°C)**
- **Small flan dish**

| | | |
|---|---|---|
| 1 tbsp | pale muscovado sugar | 15 mL |
| 3 oz | curd or cream cheese | 90 g |
| 1 | large egg | 1 |
| ¼ cup | milk | 60 mL |
| | Grated zest and juice of 2 lemons, divided | |
| 2 tbsp | sliced almonds | 30 mL |
| 6 tbsp | plain Greek yogurt | 90 mL |
| 1 tsp | liquid honey | 5 mL |

1. In a bowl, beat the sugar, cheese, egg, milk, half of the lemon zest and half of the lemon juice.

2. Pour the batter into the flan dish. Sprinkle the almonds over top.

3. Bake in preheated oven for 35 minutes or until a tester inserted in the center comes out clean.

4. Remove the cake from the oven and let cool completely in the pan on a wire rack.

5. In a bowl, beat the yogurt, honey and the remaining lemon zest and juice until well combined.

6. Drizzle each portion of cheesecake with yogurt sauce.

# Chocolate Plum Cake

This is a lovely cake when fresh plums are in season, but at other times you can use soft prunes. If you are making it with prunes, reduce the sugar to 6 tbsp (90 mL), as prunes are much sweeter than plums.

## Tip

When it has cooled to room temperature, you can cut the cake in half horizontally and fill it with a layer of good-quality plum jam.

### NUTRIENTS PER SERVING

| | |
|---|---|
| Calories | 231 |
| Carbohydrate | 23 g |
| Fiber | 4 g |
| Protein | 4 g |
| Fat | 15 g |
| Saturated fat | 9 g |
| Cholesterol | 68 mg |
| Sodium | 146 mg |

**Food Choices**

| | |
|---|---|
| 1 | Carbohydrate |
| 2½ | Fat |

- **Preheat oven to 350°F (180°C)**
- **Mini chopper or food processor**
- **6-inch (15 cm) round cake pan, bottom lined with parchment paper, bottom and sides greased**

| | | |
|---|---|---|
| ¾ cup | quick-cooking rolled oats | 175 mL |
| ⅓ cup | whole wheat flour | 75 mL |
| 4 | ripe fresh plums, pitted, or soft prunes | 4 |
| ½ cup | butter or reduced-fat margarine | 125 mL |
| ½ cup | dark muscovado sugar | 125 mL |
| ½ cup | unsweetened cocoa powder | 125 mL |
| 2 | large eggs | 2 |
| 1 tsp | baking powder | 5 mL |
| 1½ oz | dark chocolate (65% to 75% cacao), finely chopped | 45 g |

1. In the mini chopper or food processor, process oats to a coarse powder.

2. In a small bowl, combine the oat powder and flour. Set aside.

3. In a medium bowl, mash three of the plums or prunes until smooth (or purée them in the clean food processor). Chop the remaining plum or prune into fairly small pieces.

4. In a large bowl, using an electric mixer, beat the butter and sugar until light and fluffy. Beat in the cocoa powder, then the mashed plums. Beat in the eggs, one at a time, each with a spoonful of the oat mixture.

5. Using a wooden spoon, stir in the remaining oat mixture and the baking powder until just combined. Fold in the chocolate and the chopped plum or prune. Spoon into the prepared pan.

6. Bake in preheated oven for 40 minutes or until a tester inserted in the center comes out clean.

7. Remove the cake from the oven and let cool in the pan on a wire cooling rack for 10 minutes. Turn the cake out onto the rack to cool completely.

# Rich Seedy Cake

This classic seedy cake makes several servings, so you may want to freeze half of it. Make sure to wrap it well; otherwise, it will dry out. Let it thaw overnight in the refrigerator.

## Tip

Because this cake is high in fat, it should be a special occasion treat on days when your fat consumption is otherwise low.

## Variation

Use whole wheat flour instead of all-purpose flour.

### NUTRIENTS PER SERVING

| | |
|---|---|
| Calories | 238 |
| Carbohydrate | 16 g |
| Fiber | 0 g |
| Protein | 4 g |
| Fat | 17 g |
| Saturated fat | 10 g |
| Cholesterol | 103 mg |
| Sodium | 159 mg |

#### Food Choices

| | |
|---|---|
| 2 | Carbohydrate |
| 3 | Fat |

- **Preheat the oven to 350°F (180°C)**
- **8- by 4-inch (20 by 10 cm) loaf pan, bottom lined with parchment paper, bottom and sides greased**

| ½ cup | butter or reduced-fat margarine, softened | 125 mL |
|---|---|---|
| 6 tbsp | pale muscovado sugar | 90 mL |
| 2 | large eggs, separated | 2 |
| 1 tsp | caraway seeds | 5 mL |
| ½ tsp | ground cinnamon | 2 mL |
| ½ tsp | ground nutmeg | 2 mL |
| 1 cup | sifted all-purpose flour | 250 mL |

1. In a large bowl, using an electric mixer, beat the butter and sugar until light and fluffy.

2. Beat in the egg yolks, one at a time, then beat in the caraway seeds, cinnamon and nutmeg until well combined.

3. In a small bowl, whisk the egg whites until they just hold their shape. Using a spatula, fold them into the batter.

4. Fold the flour into the batter until well combined. Spoon the batter into the prepared pan.

5. Bake in preheated oven for 40 minutes or until a tester inserted in the center comes out clean.

6. Remove the cake from the oven and let cool in the pan on a wire cooling rack for 10 minutes. Turn the cake out onto the rack to cool completely.

# Lemon Poppy Seed Cake

This small loaf cake will freeze well for future use. However, if you are going to freeze it, wait until it has been thawed before icing it.

## Tip

Because this cake is high in fat, it should be a special occasion treat on days when your fat consumption is otherwise low.

- **Preheat oven to 350°F (180°C)**
- **8- by 4-inch (20 by 10 cm) loaf pan, bottom lined with parchment paper, bottom and sides greased**

| | | |
|---|---|---|
| 1¼ cups | all-purpose flour, sifted | 300 mL |
| 1 tbsp | poppy seeds | 15 mL |
| 1¾ tsp | baking powder | 8 mL |
| ¼ tsp | salt | 1 mL |
| | Grated zest of 1 lemon | |
| ¾ cup | unsalted butter or reduced-fat margarine | 175 mL |
| ¾ cup | xylitol, granulated sugar or pale muscovado sugar | 175 mL |
| 2 | large eggs | 2 |
| 3 tbsp | freshly squeezed lemon juice (approx.), divided | 45 mL |
| 2 tbsp | confectioners' (icing) sugar | 30 mL |

1. In a small bowl, whisk together the flour, poppy seeds, baking powder, salt and lemon zest. Set aside.

2. In a large bowl, using an electric mixer, beat the butter and sugar until light and fluffy.

3. Beat in the eggs, one at a time, each with 1 tbsp (15 mL) of flour. Beat in 1½ tbsp (22 mL) of the lemon juice.

4. Spoon the batter into the prepared pan and tap the pan gently on the countertop a few times to flatten out the top.

5. Bake in preheated oven for 45 minutes or until a tester inserted in the center comes out clean.

6. Remove the cake from the oven and let cool in the pan on a wire cooling rack for 10 minutes. Turn the cake out onto the rack to cool completely.

7. In a small bowl, combine the confectioners' sugar and up to 5 tsp (25 mL) lemon juice. You want the icing to be quite thick, but spreadable.

8. Spoon the icing onto the cooled cake, then smooth it out with a spatula dipped in hot water, allowing the drips to run down the side of the cake. Let dry before cutting.

## NUTRIENTS PER SERVING

| | |
|---|---|
| Calories | 331 |
| Carbohydrate | 37 g |
| Fiber | 1 g |
| Protein | 4 g |
| Fat | 19 g |
| Saturated fat | 11 g |
| Cholesterol | 92 mg |
| Sodium | 161 mg |

### Food Choices

| | |
|---|---|
| 2½ | Carbohydrate |
| 3½ | Fat |

# Xylitol

Xylitol not only has a very low glycemic index, but it is also low in calories, so it's great for weight control. It can be substituted in equal amounts for granulated sugar. Although it does not deliver the same flavor as, say, muscovado sugar, it allows you to have a sweet cake without sending your blood sugars rocketing.

# Upside-Down Fruitcake

<table>
<tr><td colspan="3">Makes 4 servings</td></tr>
</table>

This cake is the perfect solution for those who cannot tolerate the amount of sugar delivered by a regular fruitcake. The combination of flours gives it an interesting texture. It is delicious warm or cold.

● **Small springform pan**

| | | |
|---|---|---|
| 1 | small apple, peeled and sliced | 1 |
| 1 | soft date, chopped | 1 |
| ½ tsp | raisins | 2 mL |
| Pinch | ground cinnamon | Pinch |
| Pinch | ground ginger | Pinch |
| Pinch | ground cloves | Pinch |
| Pinch | ground nutmeg | Pinch |
| 1 tsp | brandy (optional) | 5 mL |
| | Grated zest and juice of ½ lemon | |
| ¼ cup | rice flour | 60 mL |
| ½ tsp | baking powder | 2 mL |
| ¼ cup | cornmeal | 60 mL |
| 2 tbsp | butter or coconut oil | 30 mL |
| 2 tbsp | pale muscovado sugar | 30 mL |
| 1 | large egg | 1 |

1. In a small bowl, combine the apple, date, raisins, cinnamon, ginger, cloves, nutmeg, brandy (if using), lemon zest and half of the lemon juice. Stir well, until the fruit is well coated in the spices and the liquid. Cover and let steep for 1 to 3 hours.

2. Preheat the oven to 350°F (180°C). Line the springform pan with foil and lightly grease the foil and the sides of the pan.

3. Spread the fruit mixture over the bottom of the prepared pan, flattening it out as much as possible.

4. Sift the rice flour and baking powder into a small bowl. Stir in the cornmeal. Set aside.

5. In a large bowl, using an electric mixer, beat the butter and sugar until light and fluffy.

## NUTRIENTS PER SERVING

| | |
|---|---|
| Calories | 189 |
| Carbohydrate | 30 g |
| Fiber | 1 g |
| Protein | 3 g |
| Fat | 7 g |
| Saturated fat | 4 g |
| Cholesterol | 62 mg |
| Sodium | 108 mg |

### Food Choices

| | |
|---|---|
| 1½ | Carbohydrate |
| 1 | Fat |
| 1 | Extra |

6. Using a wooden spoon, beat in the egg, along with a little flour mixture. Fold in the rest of the flour and the remaining lemon juice.

7. Spoon the batter into the pan and tap the pan gently on the countertop a few times to flatten out the top.

8. Bake in preheated oven for 20 to 25 minutes or until a tester inserted in the center comes out clean.

9. Remove the cake from the oven, run a knife around the edge of the pan, then remove the sides of the pan. Using the foil, carefully lift the cake off the pan bottom and invert it onto a serving dish. Carefully peel off the foil and turn the cake right side up. Let cool slightly or completely.

# Seriously Nutty Fruitcake

**Makes
12 servings**

This cake is loaded with nuts and uses bananas as a sweetener. It keeps well, so you can wrap half tightly and freeze it.

## Tips

Apricots, of which there are lots in this cake, are one of the lowest dried fruits on the glycemic index and have a very low glycemic load.

The cake can be quite crumbly if you try to cut it before it has cooled completely.

- **Preheat oven to 325°F (160°C)**
- **Mini chopper (optional)**
- **Food processor**
- **6-inch (15 cm) cake pan, bottom lined with parchment paper, bottom and sides greased**

| | | |
|---|---|---|
| ¾ cup | quick-cooking rolled oats | 175 mL |
| ⅔ cup | all-purpose flour | 150 mL |
| 2 tsp | baking powder | 10 mL |
| 2 tsp | ground nutmeg | 10 mL |
| 1 tsp | ground cinnamon | 5 mL |
| 1 tsp | ground ginger | 5 mL |
| 2 | ripe bananas | 2 |
| ½ cup | butter, reduced-fat margarine or coconut oil | 125 mL |
| | Grated zest and juice of 2 lemons | |
| 2 | large eggs, lightly beaten | 2 |
| ½ cup | raisins | 125 mL |
| ½ cup | sultana raisins | 125 mL |
| ¾ cup | soft dried apricots, chopped roughly | 175 mL |
| ½ cup | chopped walnuts or pecans | 125 mL |
| ½ cup | toasted hazelnuts, chopped roughly | 125 mL |
| ¼ cup | sliced almonds | 60 mL |
| ¼ cup | pine nuts | 60 mL |
| 2 tbsp | brandy, orange juice or apple juice | 30 mL |

1. In the mini chopper or the food processor, process oats to a coarse powder.
2. In a small bowl, combine the oat powder, flour, baking powder, nutmeg, cinnamon and ginger. Set aside.

## NUTRIENTS PER SERVING

| | |
|---|---|
| Calories | 308 |
| Carbohydrate | 33 g |
| Fiber | 4 g |
| Protein | 6 g |
| Fat | 18 g |
| Saturated fat | 6 g |
| Cholesterol | 51 mg |
| Sodium | 135 mg |

### Food Choices

| | |
|---|---|
| 2 | Carbohydrate |
| 3 | Fat |

3. In the food processor, purée the banana, butter, lemon zest and lemon juice until smooth.

4. Transfer the banana mixture to a large bowl and stir in the eggs. Stir in the raisins, sultana raisins, apricots, walnuts, hazelnuts, almonds and pine nuts. Stir in the flour mixture until well combined. Stir in the brandy. Spoon the mixture into the prepared pan and smooth the top.

5. Bake in preheated oven for 1 hour or until a tester inserted in the center comes out clean.

6. Remove the cake from the oven and let cool in the pan on a wire cooling rack for 10 minutes. Turn the cake out onto the rack to cool completely.

# Strawberry Oat Crumble

This new take on crumble is a great way to use up fruit that is a bit squashed or over-ripe. It is good both hot and cold, so make enough for two even if you are on your own. Serve it on its own or with yogurt.

- **Preheat oven to 350°F (180°C)**
- **Food processor or blender**
- **Small, shallow baking dish or flan dish (at least 1/2 inch/1 cm deep)**

| | | |
|---|---|---|
| ¾ cup | large-flake (old-fashioned) or quick cooking rolled oats | 175 mL |
| ¼ cup | coarse cornmeal or whole wheat flour | 60 mL |
| 2 tbsp | coconut oil or butter, melted | 30 mL |
| 1 tbsp | agave syrup | 15 mL |
| 1½ cups | strawberries or raspberries | 375 mL |
| 1 tsp | arrowroot starch | 5 mL |

1. In a bowl, combine the oats, cornmeal, butter and agave syrup.

2. In the food processor or blender, purée half of the strawberries. Roughly chop the remaining strawberries (if using raspberries, you can skip the chopping).

3. In a small pan, combine the arrowroot starch and a little bit of the purée; stir until smooth. Stir in the remaining purée. Heat over medium-low heat until thickened. Stir in the chopped strawberries.

4. Spread half of the oat mixture over the bottom of the baking dish. Spread the strawberry mixture over the crumble and the rest of the oat mixture over the strawberries.

5. Bake in preheated oven for 30 minutes or until the filling is bubbling and the topping is golden brown. Serve warm or cold.

## NUTRIENTS PER SERVING

| | |
|---|---|
| Calories | 360 |
| Carbohydrate | 50 g |
| Fiber | 6 g |
| Protein | 6 g |
| Fat | 16 g |
| Saturated fat | 12 g |
| Cholesterol | 0 mg |
| Sodium | 9 mg |

### Food Choices

| | |
|---|---|
| 3 | Carbohydrate |
| 3 | Fat |

# Coconut Oil

Coconut oil is a good substitute for butter. Although it is just as high in saturated fat, the saturated fat in coconut oil is largely medium-chain triglycerides, which are helpful for weight loss and atherosclerosis as well as blood sugar control.

# Apple Berry Crumble

**Makes 2 servings**

Make enough for two, as this dessert keeps well and is delicious cold. Serve it on its own or with yogurt.

## Tip

If you want to avoid using sweetener, substitute 2 fresh dates for the cane sugar. Add them with the fruit and water before cooking, and mash the mixture once dates are softened. The dates will provide sweetness, but in a much more diabetes-friendly manner, as they are high in fiber.

**NUTRIENTS PER SERVING**

| | |
|---|---|
| Calories | 220 |
| Carbohydrate | 44 g |
| Fiber | 9 g |
| Protein | 5 g |
| Fat | 5 g |
| Saturated fat | 1 g |
| Cholesterol | 0 mg |
| Sodium | 6 mg |

**Food Choices**

| | |
|---|---|
| 2 | Carbohydrate |

- **Preheat oven to 350°F (180°C)**
- **Small pie dish**

| | | |
|---|---|---|
| 1 | large tart cooking apple (such as Granny Smith, Crispin or Northern Spy) or other seasonal fruit | 1 |
| 1½ cups | mixed berries or red currants (or a combination) | 375 mL |
| 4 to 6 tbsp | water | 60 to 90 mL |
| ½ to 1 tbsp | raw cane sugar, dark (cooking) molasses or agave syrup (optional) | 7 to 15 mL |
| ½ cup | large-flake (old-fashioned) or quick-cooking rolled oats | 125 mL |
| 1 tbsp | sliced almonds, sliced pine nuts and/or chopped pistachios | 15 mL |

1. Cut the apple or other fruit into small pieces, leaving the skin on. Trim or stem the currants, if using.

2. Transfer the fruit to a saucepan and add the water. Cover and bring to a boil. Reduce the heat and simmer for 5 minutes or until the apple is nearly tender. Taste and, if necessary, sweeten to taste with sugar. Transfer to the pie dish.

3. In a bowl, combine the oats and nuts. Spread over the fruit.

4. Bake in preheated oven for 30 minutes or until the topping is lightly browned. Serve hot, warm or at room temperature.

# Hot Plum Dessert

**Makes 4 servings**

Mixing just a few prunes in with the fresh plums gives you a little sugar boost without pushing up the sugar content of the dish too much. Chickpea flour contributes a nutty texture and taste. This is another dessert that tastes good cold.

## Tip

Because this dessert is high in fat, it should be a special occasion treat on days when your fat consumption is otherwise low.

**NUTRIENTS PER SERVING**

| | |
|---|---|
| Calories | 204 |
| Carbohydrate | 17 g |
| Fiber | 2 g |
| Protein | 5 g |
| Fat | 13 g |
| Saturated fat | 8 g |
| Cholesterol | 71 mg |
| Sodium | 163 mg |

**Food Choices**

| | |
|---|---|
| 2 | Carbohydrate |
| 2½ | Fat |

### • Small pie plate

| | | |
|---|---|---|
| 4 | small plums, divided | 4 |
| 2 | prunes | 2 |
| ½ cup | chickpea (gram) flour | 125 mL |
| ½ tsp | baking powder | 2 mL |
| ¼ cup | butter | 60 mL |
| 2 tbsp | dark muscovado sugar or agave syrup | 30 mL |
| 1 | egg | 1 |

1. Place 2 plums and the prunes in a small saucepan. Cover and cook over very low heat, stirring regularly, for 30 minutes or until the fruit has cooked down into a marmalade-like sauce.

2. Preheat the oven to 350°F (180°C).

3. Remove the stones from the cooked plum mixture and spread the mixture in the bottom of the pie plate.

4. Halve the remaining plums and remove the stones. Arrange them cut side up over the cooked plum mixture.

5. Sift the chickpea flour and baking powder into a small bowl. Set aside.

6. In a medium bowl, using an electric mixer, beat the butter and sugar until light and fluffy. Beat in the egg, along with a spoonful of the flour mixture.

7. Using a wooden spoon, fold in the remaining flour mixture. Spoon the mixture over the plums.

8. Bake in preheated oven for 30 to 35 minutes or until a tester inserted in the center comes out clean.

9. Let cool slightly, then serve the pudding straight from the pie plate or loosen the edges and turn it out onto a serving dish.

# Apple and Cranberry Clafouti

This clafouti tastes good cold as well as hot, so make enough for two even if you are on your own.

## Tips

Nut milk (almond or hazelnut) gives the clafouti an added dimension of flavor.

Baking mellows cranberries, so they don't taste so bitter.

- **Preheat the oven to 350°F (180°C)**
- **Flan dish**

| | | |
|---|---|---|
| 2 | soft dates, pitted and cut into thin slivers | 2 |
| 1 | large tart cooking apple (such as Granny Smith, Crispin or Northern Spy), peeled and sliced | 1 |
| ½ cup | fresh cranberries | 125 mL |
| 1 | large egg | 1 |
| ½ cup | milk (cow's, unsweetened soy, oat or nut) | 125 mL |
| 1 tsp | orange-flavored liqueur (such as Grand Marnier) or agave syrup | 5 mL |

1. In the flan dish, combine the dates, apple and cranberries.

2. In a small bowl, beat the egg, then whisk in the milk and liqueur. Pour over the fruit.

3. Bake in preheated oven for 30 to 40 minutes or until the custard is set. Serve warm or at room temperature.

## NUTRIENTS PER SERVING

| | |
|---|---|
| Calories | 212 |
| Carbohydrate | 39 g |
| Fiber | 4 g |
| Protein | 6 g |
| Fat | 5 g |
| Saturated fat | 2 g |
| Cholesterol | 99 mg |
| Sodium | 63 mg |

### Food Choices

| | |
|---|---|
| 2 | Carbohydrate |
| 1 | Fat |

# Pears with Chocolate and Ginger Wine Sauce

**Makes 1 serving**

## Tip

If ginger wine is not available, substitute 2 slices peeled gingerroot, ½ tsp (2 mL) liquid honey and ¼ cup (60 mL) white wine or apple juice. Simmer in the saucepan for 5 minutes before adding the pear. Remove the gingerroot before stirring the cooking liquid into the chocolate mixture. Alternatively, you can use ¼ cup (60 mL) ginger beer.

| | | |
|---|---|---|
| 1 | small, slightly under-ripe pear | 1 |
| ¼ cup | ginger wine (see tip, at left) | 60 mL |
| 1 oz | dark chocolate (70% to 85% cacao), broken into small pieces | 30 g |
| 2 tbsp | half-and-half (10%) cream (or soy or oat cream) | 30 mL |

1. Carefully peel the pear, leaving it whole. Place it in the bottom of a small saucepan and pour the wine around it. Cover and bring to a simmer over medium heat. Reduce heat to low and simmer for 15 minutes or until the pear is tender.

2. Meanwhile, in another small saucepan, combine the chocolate and cream. Heat over low heat, stirring regularly, until the chocolate is melted. Remove from the heat.

3. Using a slotted spoon, transfer the pear to a serving dish. Stir the ginger wine into the chocolate mixture and let cool slightly.

4. With a spoon, carefully drizzle some of the chocolate sauce over the pear so that it drips down the sides. Spoon the rest of the sauce into the bottom of the dish. Serve at room temperature.

## NUTRIENTS PER SERVING

| | |
|---|---|
| Calories | 342 |
| Carbohydrate | 38 g |
| Fiber | 8 g |
| Protein | 4 g |
| Fat | 15 g |
| Saturated fat | 7 g |
| Cholesterol | 12 mg |
| Sodium | 15 mg |

### Food Choices

| | |
|---|---|
| 2 | Carbohydrate |
| 3 | Fat |

# Hot Fruit Salad

**Makes 6 servings**

You can leave this old-fashioned compote in the fridge for weeks and just dip in when you feel inclined — the flavors get better as they mature. Serve warm or cold with yogurt or your favorite breakfast cereal.

| | | |
|---|---|---|
| 1 lb | mixed unsweetened dried fruit (apricots, apples, prunes, large raisins, sultanas, figs, pears) | 500 g |
| ¼ cup | red wine or unsweetened pomegranate or orange juice | 60 mL |
| 1 | 3-inch (7.5 cm) cinnamon stick (or 1 tsp/5 mL ground cinnamon) | 1 |
| | Grated zest of 1 small lemon | |

1. If the fruit is very dry, soak it overnight, then drain it and discard the water.

2. In a large saucepan, combine dried fruit, 1¾ cups (425 mL) water, wine, cinnamon and lemon zest. Bring to a simmer over medium-low heat, then reduce heat and simmer gently for 10 to 15 minutes or until fruit is tender.

3. Using a slotted spoon, transfer the fruit to a bowl. Continue to simmer the juice for 20 minutes or until thickened and slightly reduced. Pour the sauce over the fruit.

**NUTRIENTS PER SERVING**

| | |
|---|---|
| Calories | 238 |
| Carbohydrate | 60 g |
| Fiber | 6 g |
| Protein | 2 g |
| Fat | 0 g |
| Saturated fat | 0 g |
| Cholesterol | 0 mg |
| Sodium | 20 mg |

**Food Choices**

3½ Carbohydrates

# Dried Fruits

Although they contain a good deal of natural sugar, dried fruits have a relatively low glycemic load because they also contain significant amounts of fiber and nutrients. Provided you do not use sweetened dried fruits, or add any sugar to the recipe, they are perfectly acceptable in a diabetes-management diet.

# Coconut Milk Crème

This delicious recipe is perfect for those trying to avoid dairy products and sugar. The classic burnt sugar topping is replaced with toasted almonds — even better! Make yourself a single portion whenever you feel like a treat.

- **Preheat oven to 300°F (150°C)**
- **¾-cup (175 mL) ramekin**

| | | |
|---|---|---|
| 6 tbsp | light coconut milk | 90 mL |
| ¼ | vanilla bean, split (or ¼ tsp/1 mL vanilla extract) | ¼ |
| ½ tsp | agave syrup (optional) | 2 mL |
| 1 | large egg yolk | 1 |
| 1 tsp | sliced almonds | 5 mL |

1. In a small saucepan, over medium heat, heat the coconut milk and vanilla bean until just about to boil. Remove the vanilla pod and taste the coconut milk. If you would like it slightly sweeter, add the agave syrup.

2. In a small bowl, using a fork, whisk the egg yolk thoroughly. Whisking constantly, gradually add the hot coconut milk. Pour into the ramekin.

3. Bake in preheated oven for 20 to 30 minutes or until just set. Let cool slightly.

4. Meanwhile, in a dry frying pan, toast the almonds over medium heat, stirring constantly, until fragrant and lightly browned.

5. Spread the almonds over the top of the custard. Serve at room temperature or refrigerate until chilled.

## NUTRIENTS PER SERVING

| | |
|---|---|
| Calories | 139 |
| Carbohydrate | 5 g |
| Fiber | 0 g |
| Protein | 3 g |
| Fat | 11 g |
| Saturated fat | 6 g |
| Cholesterol | 184 mg |
| Sodium | 13 mg |

### Food Choices

| | |
|---|---|
| 2 | Fat |
| 1 | Extra |

# Coconut Milk

Coconut milk is naturally sweet, yet has a low glycemic load. Although it is high in saturated fat, the fat is in the form of medium-chain triglycerides, which are now recognized to be very helpful with weight control, atherosclerosis and cardiovascular disease and to have a slight blood-glucose-lowering effect.

# Chocolate Pots

This easy recipe tastes so good, you'll keep coming back to it. Even if you are on your own, make enough for two, as it will sit happily in the fridge for a couple of days.

- **Two ¾-cup (175 mL) ramekins**

| | | |
|---|---|---|
| 2 tsp | cornstarch | 10 mL |
| ½ cup | milk (cow's, soy, oat or rice) | 125 mL |
| 1 oz | dark chocolate (65% to 75% cacao), broken into small pieces | 30 g |
| | Berries, confectioners' (icing) sugar or grated dark chocolate | |

1. Place the cornstarch in a small saucepan and gradually stir in the milk until the mixture is a smooth paste. Heat over medium-low heat, stirring constantly, until thickened.

2. Add the chocolate and stir until melted. Pour into the ramekins, cover and refrigerate until chilled.

3. Serve decorated with berries, confectioners' sugar or a little grated chocolate.

## NUTRIENTS PER SERVING

| | |
|---|---|
| Calories | 113 |
| Carbohydrate | 12 g |
| Fiber | 1 g |
| Protein | 3 g |
| Fat | 8 g |
| Saturated fat | 4 g |
| Cholesterol | 6 mg |
| Sodium | 26 mg |

### Food Choices

| | |
|---|---|
| 1 | Carbohydrate |
| 1½ | Fat |

# Chocolate Strawberries

This incredibly simple dessert can really give a lift to a meal on your own and is also fun for two. Pick strawberries that have good stems to hold on to while you are dipping.

## Tip

Dark chocolate (the darker the better) is low on the glycemic index as it has relatively little sugar — but it delivers a great chocolate hit!

| 2 oz | dark chocolate (65% to 75% cacao), chopped | 60 g |
|------|---------------------------------------------|------|
| 6 | strawberries | 6 |

1. In a small saucepan, melt the chocolate over low heat.

2. Set out a rack to receive the strawberries. Holding a strawberry by the stem, dip it in the chocolate, covering the end, the side or as much of the strawberry as you like. Place the strawberry on the rack. Repeat with the remaining strawberries.

3. Let the chocolate cool and harden for 2 to 3 hours (or go ahead and eat the strawberries immediately if you can't stand to wait).

---

**NUTRIENTS PER SERVING**

| | |
|---|---|
| Calories | 152 |
| Carbohydrate | 18 g |
| Fiber | 4 g |
| Protein | 3 g |
| Fat | 11 g |
| Saturated fat | 7 g |
| Cholesterol | 0 mg |
| Sodium | 0 mg |

**Food Choices**

| 1 | Carbohydrate |
|---|---|
| 2 | Fat |

# About the Nutrient Analyses

THE NUTRIENT ANALYSIS done on the recipes in chapters 1, 2, 3 and 6 was derived from The Nutrition Company, FoodWorks Software Nutrition Analysis Program, version 15.0. The nutrient analysis done on the recipes in chapters 4 and 5 was derived from the Food Processor SQL Nutrition Analysis Software, version 10.9, ESHA Research (2011). Where necessary, data was supplemented using the following references: 1) The Canadian Nutrient File (2010); 2) USDA National Nutrient Database for Standard Reference, Release #26 (2014); 3) Helpful Hints for Educators Using Beyond the Basics: Meal Planning for Healthy Eating, Diabetes Prevention and Management (2013); 4) Revised Longer Lists of Foods To Be Used with Beyond the Basics: Meal Planning for Healthy Eating, Diabetes Prevention and Management, Version 2 (2005); 5) Assigning Canadian Diabetes Association Food Choice Values (Food Intelligence, 2012).

Recipes were evaluated as follows:

- Where alternatives are given, the first ingredient and amount listed were used.
- Optional ingredients and ingredients that are not quantified were not included.
- Calculations were based on imperial measures and weights.
- The smaller quantity of an ingredient was used where a range is provided.
- Calculations involving meat and poultry used lean portions.
- Recipes were analyzed prior to cooking.
- A pinch of salt was analyzed as 1/16 tsp (0.3 mL).
- Where canned beans are used, they are assumed to be rinsed very thoroughly, thereby removing about one-third of the sodium listed on the can.
- Nutrient values were rounded to the nearest whole number.

It is important to note that the cooking method used to prepare the recipe may alter the nutrient content and food choice assignments per serving, as may ingredient substitutions and differences among brand-name products.

# About the Food Choices

FOOD CHOICES ASSIGNMENTS were based on the Canadian Diabetes Association food choice values in the table below. Available carbohydrate is total carbohydrate minus fiber.

## Food Choice Values

| FOOD CHOICE | AVAILABLE CARBOHYDRATE | PROTEIN | FAT |
|---|---|---|---|
| *Carbohydrate* | | | |
| Grains and Starches | 15 g | 3 g | 0 g |
| Fruits | 15 g | 1 g | 0 g |
| Milk and Alternatives | 15 g | 8 g | 0 g |
| Other Choices | 15 g | variable | variable |
| Vegetables | <5 g (most) Not usually counted in Carbohydrate Choices | 2 g | 0 g |
| *Meat and Alternatives* | 0 g | 7 g | 3–5 g |
| *Fat* | 0 g | 0 g | 5 g |

Adapted from *Beyond the Basics: Meal Planning for Healthy Eating, Diabetes Prevention and Management.* © Canadian Diabetes Association, 2005.

# Index

## A

Ajwar, 22
almonds
  Baked Lemon and Almond
    Cheesecake, 119
  Lemon Shortbread, 116
anchovies, 39
  Beef and Mushroom Casserole,
    100
  Chicken with Anchovies and
    Cauliflower, 76
  Fusilli with Capers and
    Anchovies, 54
  Pepper, Pear and Anchovy Salad,
    38
  Stir-Fried Tuna with Snow Peas,
    68
apples
  Apple and Cranberry Clafouti,
    132
  Apple Berry Crumble, 130
  Baked Trout with Apple, 64
  Chicken and Apple Salad, 37
  Kale with Beet Leaves, 45
  Pork Chops with Apple, 97
  Red Cabbage Casserole, 44
  Stewed or Baked Apple, 97
  Tuna with Beets and Red
    Cabbage, 66
  Upside-Down Fruitcake, 124
artichoke hearts, 81
  Chicken with Artichoke Hearts,
    80
avocado, 31
  Chicken with Avocado and Earl
    Grey Tea, 84
  Spinach, Avocado and Mozzarella
    Salad, 30

## B

bacon
  Coffee-Infused Beef Stew, 102
  Rack of Lamb with Mustard
    Crust, 106
balsamic vinegar, 43
bananas, 113
  Banana and Polenta Bread, 112
  Seriously Nutty Fruitcake, 126
beans
  Beef with Curly Kale, 104
  Beet and Chickpea Salad, 36
  Herb Frittata, 86
  Pork Chops with Beets and
    Butter Beans, 94
  Sausage and Bean Pot, 92
  Watercress Soup, 14
beef
  Beef and Mushroom Casserole,
    100
  Beef Casserole with Butternut
    Squash, 101
  Beef with Curly Kale, 104
  Bobotie, 103

Coffee-Infused Beef Stew, 102
  Slow-Cooked Pot Roast, 98
  Steak with Garlic, 99
beets and beet greens, 67
  Beet and Chickpea Salad, 36
  Kale with Beet Leaves, 45
  Pork Chops with Beets and
    Butter Beans, 94
  Tuna with Beets and Red
    Cabbage, 66
berries
  Apple and Cranberry Clafouti,
    132
  Apple Berry Crumble, 130
  Chocolate Strawberries, 139
  Fennel and Strawberry Salad, 32
  Strawberry Oat Crumble, 128
  Whole Wheat Blueberry Muffins,
    114
Bobotie, 103
bread (as ingredient)
  Ajwar, 22
  Bobotie, 103
Brussels Sprout and Celery Root
  Salad, 28
Butternut Squash and Baked Eggs,
  88

## C

cabbage
  Pork Medallions with Lentils and
    Cabbage, 96
  Red Cabbage Casserole, 44
  Tuna with Beets and Red
    Cabbage, 66
cakes, 119–26
carrots
  Beef with Curly Kale, 104
  Carrot and Red Lentil Soup, 15
  Chicken with Artichoke Hearts,
    80
  Lamb Tagine, 108
  Slow-Cooked Pot Roast, 98
cauliflower, 77
  Cauliflower and Cashew Salad,
    29
  Chicken with Anchovies and
    Cauliflower, 76
  Pasta and Broccoli au Gratin,
    51
celery. See also celery root
  Chicken and Lentil Soup, 19
  Chicken with Artichoke Hearts,
    80
  Lamb Tagine, 108
  New Orleans Jambalaya, 71
  Salmon with Asian Greens, 62
  Sausage and Bean Pot, 92
celery root
  Beef with Curly Kale, 104
  Brussels Sprout and Celery Root
    Salad, 28
  Celery Root Soup with Salmon,
    18

Celery Root with Kale and
    Pecans, 46
  Haddock Chowder, 16
cheese
  Baked Lemon and Almond
    Cheesecake, 119
  Pasta and Broccoli au Gratin, 51
  Ratatouille with Butternut
    Squash, 48
  Spinach, Avocado and Mozzarella
    Salad, 30
chicken
  Chicken and Apple Salad, 37
  Chicken and Lentil Soup, 19
  Chicken and Okra Savory, 20
  Chicken Salad with Pumpkin
    Oil, 42
  Chicken with Anchovies and
    Cauliflower, 76
  Chicken with Artichoke Hearts,
    80
  Chicken with Avocado and Earl
    Grey Tea, 84
  Chicken with Ginger and Water
    Chestnuts, 85
  New Orleans Jambalaya, 71
  Oven-Baked Chicken with Split
    Peas, 74
  Pan-Fried Chicken with Okra, 78
  Pomegranate Chicken, 82
  Second-Day Chicken Soup, 75
  Simple Marinade for Lamb,
    Chicken or Fish, 82
chickpea flour
  Chocolate Brownies, 118
  Hot Plum Dessert, 131
chickpeas. See also chickpea flour
  Beet and Chickpea Salad, 36
  Chickpeas with Peppers and
    Chard, 50
  Lamb Tagine, 108
chocolate
  Chocolate Brownies, 118
  Chocolate Plum Cake, 120
  Chocolate Pots, 138
  Chocolate Strawberries, 139
  Coffee-Infused Beef Stew, 102
  Pears with Chocolate and Ginger
    Wine Sauce, 133
Cinnamon Oat Squares, 117
cocoa powder. See chocolate
coconut milk, 137
  Coconut Milk Crème, 136
  Cod with Clams and Coconut
    Milk, 58
coconut oil, 129
Cod with Clams and Coconut
  Milk, 58
Coffee-Infused Beef Stew, 102
cookies and squares, 115–18
cornmeal
  Banana and Polenta Bread, 112
  Upside-Down Fruitcake, 124
Cracked Wheat with Spinach and
  Pine Nuts, 49

cream. *See also* milk
  Eggs au Miroir, 23
  Fettuccine with Smoked Salmon
    and Cream Sauce, 63
  Pears with Chocolate and Ginger
    Wine Sauce, 133
  Poached Trout with Rhubarb
    Sauce, 65
Cream of Mushroom Soup, 12

## D

dates
  Apple and Cranberry Clafouti,
    132
  Upside-Down Fruitcake, 124

## E

eggplant
  Ajwar, 22
  Lamb Tagine, 108
eggs
  Bobotie, 103
  Butternut Squash and Baked
    Eggs, 88
  Eggs au Miroir, 23
  Hard-Cooked Eggs with Spinach,
    24
  Herb Frittata, 86
  Lentil and Egg Pie, 89
endive (Belgian)
  Chicken Salad with Pumpkin
    Oil, 42
  Hard-Cooked Eggs with Spinach,
    24

## F

fennel (bulb)
  Fennel and Strawberry Salad, 32
  Fillet of Cod with Chiles, 60
  Fresh Seafood Salad, 40
  Leek and Fennel Soup, 10
  Salmon Steamed with Fennel
    and Tomatoes, 61
  Spinach, Avocado and Mozzarella
    Salad, 30
  Watercress Soup, 14
Fettuccine with Smoked Salmon
  and Cream Sauce, 63
fish. *See also* anchovies; seafood
  Baked Trout with Apple, 64
  Celery Root Soup with Salmon,
    18
  Cod with Clams and Coconut
    Milk, 58
  Fettuccine with Smoked Salmon
    and Cream Sauce, 63
  Fillet of Cod with Chiles, 60
  Fish Fillets with Curly Kale, 55
  Haddock Chowder, 16
  Haddock Pie, 56
  Poached Trout with Rhubarb
    Sauce, 65
  Salmon Steamed with Fennel
    and Tomatoes, 61
  Salmon with Asian Greens, 62
  Simple Marinade for Lamb,
    Chicken or Fish, 82

Stir-Fried Tuna with Snow Peas,
  68
Tuna with Beets and Red
  Cabbage, 66
fruit, dried, 135
  Apple and Cranberry Clafouti,
    132
  Cracked Wheat with Spinach
    and Pine Nuts, 49
  Hot Fruit Salad, 134
  Hot Plum Dessert, 131
  Seriously Nutty Fruitcake, 126
  Stewed or Baked Apple, 97
  Upside-Down Fruitcake, 124
fruit, fresh. *See* berries; *specific fruits*
Fusilli with Capers and Anchovies,
  54

## G

garlic
  Chickpeas with Peppers and
    Chard, 50
  Coffee-Infused Beef Stew, 102
  Fusilli with Capers and
    Anchovies, 54
  Oven-Baked Chicken with Split
    Peas, 74
  Sausage and Bean Pot, 92
  Steak with Garlic, 99
  Stir-Fried Tuna with Snow Peas,
    68
ginger
  Beef Casserole with Butternut
    Squash, 101
  Butternut Squash and Baked
    Eggs, 88
  Chickpeas with Peppers and
    Chard, 50
  Ginger and Honey Cookies, Old-
    Fashioned, 115
  Lamb and Pepper Kebabs, 107
  Oven-Baked Chicken with Split
    Peas, 74
  Pears with Chocolate and Ginger
    Wine Sauce (tip), 133
  Stir-Fried Shrimp with Ginger,
    70
  Stir-Fried Tuna with Snow Peas,
    68
greens. *See also* kale; lettuce;
  spinach
  Brussels Sprout and Celery Root
    Salad, 28
  Chicken and Apple Salad, 37
  Chicken with Avocado and Earl
    Grey Tea, 84
  Chickpeas with Peppers and
    Chard, 50
  Herb Frittata, 86
  Kale with Beet Leaves, 45
  Salmon with Asian Greens, 62
  Stir-Fried Tuna with Snow Peas,
    68
  Watercress Soup, 14

## H

Haddock Chowder, 16
Haddock Pie, 56

ham
  Chicken and Lentil Soup, 19
  New Orleans Jambalaya, 71
Hard-Cooked Eggs with Spinach,
  24
harissa, 109
herbs (fresh)
  Baked Trout with Apple, 64
  Chicken and Apple Salad, 37
  Chicken and Okra Savory, 20
  Fillet of Cod with Chiles, 60
  Hard-Cooked Eggs with Spinach,
    24
  Herb Frittata, 86
  Pork Chops with Apple, 97
  Pork Medallions with Lentils and
    Cabbage, 96
  Rack of Lamb with Mustard
    Crust, 106
  Spaghetti and Pine Nut Salad, 33
horseradish, 95
  Brussels Sprout and Celery Root
    Salad, 28
  Pork Chops with Beets and
    Butter Beans, 94
Hot Fruit Salad, 134
Hot Plum Dessert, 131

## K

kale (curly), 105
  Beef with Curly Kale, 104
  Celery Root with Kale and
    Pecans, 46
  Fish Fillets with Curly Kale, 55
  Kale with Beet Leaves, 45
  Warm Pasta and Curly Kale
    Salad, 34

## L

lamb
  Lamb and Pepper Kebabs,
    107
  Lamb Tagine, 108
  Rack of Lamb with Mustard
    Crust, 106
  Simple Marinade for Lamb,
    Chicken or Fish, 82
leeks
  Fillet of Cod with Chiles, 60
  Haddock Pie, 56
  Herb Frittata, 86
  Leek and Fennel Soup, 10
  Spinach, Avocado and Mozzarella
    Salad, 30
lemons and lemon juice
  Baked Lemon and Almond
    Cheesecake, 119
  Bobotie, 103
  Chicken and Apple Salad, 37
  Eggs au Miroir, 23
  Ginger and Honey Cookies, Old-
    Fashioned, 115
  Lemon Poppy Seed Cake, 122
  Lemon Shortbread, 116
lentils
  Carrot and Red Lentil Soup, 15
  Chicken and Lentil Soup, 19
  Lentil and Egg Pie, 89

Pork Medallions with Lentils and
Cabbage, 96
Sausage and Bean Pot, 92
lettuce, 59
Chicken and Okra Savory, 20
Cod with Clams and Coconut
Milk, 58
Pepper, Pear and Anchovy Salad,
38
Pomegranate Chicken, 82
limes and lime juice
Lamb Tagine, 108
Stir-Fried Shrimp with Ginger,
70
Stir-Fried Tuna with Snow Peas,
68

## M

Marinade for Lamb, Chicken or
Fish, Simple, 82
milk. *See also* cream
Apple and Cranberry Clafouti,
132
Bobotie, 103
Chocolate Brownies, 118
Chocolate Pots, 138
miso, 11
Moules Marinières, 69
mushrooms, 13
Beef and Mushroom Casserole,
100
Beef with Curly Kale, 104
Chicken with Artichoke Hearts,
80
Cracked Wheat with Spinach
and Pine Nuts, 49
Cream of Mushroom Soup,
12
Fettuccine with Smoked Salmon
and Cream Sauce, 63
Fusilli with Capers and
Anchovies, 54
Lentil and Egg Pie, 89
Sausage and Bean Pot, 92
Slow-Cooked Pot Roast, 98
Stir-Fried Shrimp with Ginger,
70
Warm Pasta and Curly Kale
Salad, 34

## N

New Orleans Jambalaya, 71
nuts
Apple Berry Crumble, 130
Baked Lemon and Almond
Cheesecake, 119
Cauliflower and Cashew Salad,
29
Celery Root with Kale and
Pecans, 46
Chocolate Brownies, 118
Cracked Wheat with Spinach
and Pine Nuts, 49
Lemon Shortbread, 116
Seriously Nutty Fruitcake, 126
Spaghetti and Pine Nut Salad,
33
Stewed or Baked Apple, 97

## O

oats (rolled)
Apple Berry Crumble, 130
Chocolate Brownies, 118
Chocolate Plum Cake, 120
Cinnamon Oat Squares, 117
Seriously Nutty Fruitcake, 126
Strawberry Oat Crumble, 128
okra, 21, 79
Chicken and Okra Savory, 20
Cracked Wheat with Spinach
and Pine Nuts, 49
Pan-Fried Chicken with Okra,
78
Old-Fashioned Ginger and Honey
Cookies, 115
onions. *See also* onions, green
Baked Trout with Apple, 64
Beef and Mushroom Casserole,
100
Fish Fillets with Curly Kale, 55
Sausage and Bean Pot, 92
Slow-Cooked Pot Roast, 98
onions, green
Fresh Seafood Salad, 40
Spaghetti and Pine Nut Salad,
33
Stir-Fried Shrimp with Ginger,
70
Stir-Fried Tuna with Snow Peas,
68
oranges and orange juice
Chicken with Artichoke Hearts,
80
Chicken with Ginger and Water
Chestnuts, 85
Eggs au Miroir, 23
Ginger and Honey Cookies, Old-
Fashioned, 115
Hot Fruit Salad, 134

## P

pasta
Fettuccine with Smoked Salmon
and Cream Sauce, 63
Fusilli with Capers and
Anchovies, 54
Pasta and Broccoli au Gratin, 51
Spaghetti and Pine Nut Salad,
33
Warm Pasta and Curly Kale
Salad, 34
pears
Pears with Chocolate and Ginger
Wine Sauce, 133
Pepper, Pear and Anchovy Salad,
38
peas
Cracked Wheat with Spinach
and Pine Nuts, 49
Herb Frittata, 86
Oven-Baked Chicken with Split
Peas, 74
Stir-Fried Tuna with Snow Peas,
68
pecans, 47
Celery Root with Kale and
Pecans, 46

peppers, bell
Ajwar, 22
Beef with Curly Kale, 104
Chickpeas with Peppers and
Chard, 50
Coffee-Infused Beef Stew, 102
Lamb and Pepper Kebabs, 107
New Orleans Jambalaya, 71
Pepper, Pear and Anchovy Salad,
38
Ratatouille with Butternut
Squash, 48
peppers, chile, 41
Beef with Curly Kale, 104
Fillet of Cod with Chiles, 60
Fresh Seafood Salad, 40
New Orleans Jambalaya, 71
Stir-Fried Tuna with Snow Peas,
68
pine nuts
Cracked Wheat with Spinach
and Pine Nuts, 49
Spaghetti and Pine Nut Salad, 33
plums
Chocolate Plum Cake, 120
Hot Plum Dessert, 131
pomegranate seeds, 83
Pomegranate Chicken, 82
pork. *See also* bacon; ham
Pork Chops with Apple, 97
Pork Chops with Beets and
Butter Beans, 94
Pork Medallions with Lentils and
Cabbage, 96
Sausage and Bean Pot, 92
potatoes
Haddock Chowder, 16
Haddock Pie, 56
Rack of Lamb with Mustard
Crust, 106
Salmon Steamed with Fennel
and Tomatoes, 61
Tuna with Beets and Red
Cabbage, 66
Pot Roast, Slow-Cooked, 98
pumpkin seeds. *See* seeds

## R

Rack of Lamb with Mustard Crust,
106
raisins
Cracked Wheat with Spinach
and Pine Nuts, 49
Seriously Nutty Fruitcake, 126
Stewed or Baked Apple, 97
Upside-Down Fruitcake, 124
Ratatouille with Butternut Squash,
48
Red Cabbage Casserole, 44
Rhubarb Sauce, Poached Trout
with, 65
Rich Seedy Cake, 121
rosemary
Baked Trout with Apple, 64
Pork Chops with Apple, 97
Pork Medallions with Lentils and
Cabbage, 96
Rack of Lamb with Mustard
Crust, 106

# S

salads, 28–42
salmon
  Celery Root Soup with Salmon, 18
  Fettuccine with Smoked Salmon and Cream Sauce, 63
  Salmon Steamed with Fennel and Tomatoes, 61
  Salmon with Asian Greens, 62
Sausage and Bean Pot, 92
seafood. *See also* fish
  Cod with Clams and Coconut Milk, 58
  Fresh Seafood Salad, 40
  Moules Marinières, 69
  New Orleans Jambalaya, 71
  Stir-Fried Shrimp with Ginger, 70
seaweed, 17
  Fish Fillets with Curly Kale, 55
  Haddock Chowder, 16
Second-Day Chicken Soup, 75
seeds, 35
  Butternut Squash and Baked Eggs, 88
  Cinnamon Oat Squares, 117
  Haddock Pie, 56
  Lemon Poppy Seed Cake, 122
  Red Cabbage Casserole, 44
  Rich Seedy Cake, 121
  Spaghetti and Pine Nut Salad, 33
  Warm Pasta and Curly Kale Salad, 34
Seriously Nutty Fruitcake, 126
Simple Marinade for Lamb, Chicken or Fish, 82
Slow-Cooked Pot Roast, 98
soups, 10–19, 75
Spaghetti and Pine Nut Salad, 33
spinach, 25
  Chicken Salad with Pumpkin Oil, 42
  Cracked Wheat with Spinach and Pine Nuts, 49
  Hard-Cooked Eggs with Spinach, 24
  Herb Frittata, 86
  Lamb Tagine, 108
  Leek and Fennel Soup, 10
  Salmon Steamed with Fennel and Tomatoes, 61
  Salmon with Asian Greens, 62
  Spinach, Avocado and Mozzarella Salad, 30
sprouts, 31
  Spinach, Avocado and Mozzarella Salad, 30
squash. *See also* zucchini
  Beef Casserole with Butternut Squash, 101
  Butternut Squash and Baked Eggs, 88
  Ratatouille with Butternut Squash, 48
starters, 20–24
Steak with Garlic, 99
steaming, 57
Stewed or Baked Apple, 97
Stir-Fried Shrimp with Ginger, 70
Stir-Fried Tuna with Snow Peas, 68
strawberries
  Chocolate Strawberries, 139
  Fennel and Strawberry Salad, 32
  Strawberry Oat Crumble, 128
sunflower seeds. *See* seeds

# T

tomatoes
  Fillet of Cod with Chiles, 60
  Fresh Seafood Salad, 40
  Haddock Pie, 56
  New Orleans Jambalaya, 71
  Ratatouille with Butternut Squash, 48
  Salmon Steamed with Fennel and Tomatoes, 61
tuna
  Stir-Fried Tuna with Snow Peas, 68
  Tuna with Beets and Red Cabbage, 66

# U

Upside-Down Fruitcake, 124

# V

vegetables. *See also* greens; *specific vegetables*
  Brussels Sprout and Celery Root Salad, 28
  Pasta and Broccoli au Gratin, 51
vinegar (balsamic), 43

# W

Warm Pasta and Curly Kale Salad, 34
Water Chestnuts, Chicken with Ginger and, 85
watercress
  Chicken and Apple Salad, 37
  Herb Frittata, 86
  Watercress Soup, 14
Wheat, Cracked, with Spinach and Pine Nuts, 49
Whole Wheat Blueberry Muffins, 114
wine
  Baked Trout with Apple, 64
  Beef Casserole with Butternut Squash, 101
  Fettuccine with Smoked Salmon and Cream Sauce, 63
  Moules Marinières, 69
  Pan-Fried Chicken with Okra, 78
  Pears with Chocolate and Ginger Wine Sauce, 133
  Pork Chops with Apple, 97
  Salmon Steamed with Fennel and Tomatoes, 61
  Salmon with Asian Greens, 62
  Sausage and Bean Pot, 92

# X

xylitol, 123

# Y

yogurt
  Baked Lemon and Almond Cheesecake, 119
  Pomegranate Chicken, 82
  Red Cabbage Casserole (tip), 44
  Tuna with Beets and Red Cabbage, 66

# Z

zucchini
  Haddock Pie, 56
  Lamb and Pepper Kebabs, 107
  Pan-Fried Chicken with Okra, 78
  Ratatouille with Butternut Squash, 48

**Library and Archives Canada Cataloguing in Publication**

Berriedale-Johnson, Michelle
[Diabetic cooking for one and two]
  Delicious diabetes cooking for one or two people / Michelle Berriedale-Johnson.

Includes index.
Originally published: London : Grub Street, 2013, under title: Diabetic cooking for one and two.
ISBN 978-0-7788-0476-5 (pbk.)

1. Diabetes—Diet therapy—Recipes. 2. Cooking for one. 3. Cooking for two. 4. Cookbooks.
I. Title. II. Title: Diabetic cooking for one and two.

RC662.B44 2014          641.5'6314          C2013-908437-1